CIRCUMSTANTIAL EVIDENCE

FRANK SECICH

www.highvoltagepublishing.com

First published by High Voltage Publishing Australia 2015

www.highvoltagepublishing.com

Text copyright © Frank Secich 2015

Cover design: George Matzkov
Front cover photo: Donna Santisi
Back cover photo: Theresa Kereakes

All rights reserved. No part of this book may be reproduced or transmitted by any person or entity (including Google, Amazon or similar organizations), in any form or by any means, electronic or mechanical, including photocopying, recording, scanning or by any information storage and retrieval system, without prior permission in writing from the publisher.

The Author and the publisher would like to thank all those that supplied photographs and gave permission to reproduce copyright material in this book. Every effort has been made to contact all copyright holders, and the publisher welcomes communication from any copyright holders from whom permission was inadvertently not obtained. In such cases, we will be pleased to obtain appropriate permission and provide suitable acknowledgement in future editions.

ISBN: 978-0-646-94315-2

For

Lisa and Jake

CHAPTERS

1 - ED SULLIVAN.. THAT BASTARD RUINED EVERYTHING!
2 - GOD HAS A TREMENDOUS SENSE OF HUMOR
3 - REBELS WITHOUT A PAUSE
4 - FREE BEER!
5 - EIGHT ARMS TO HOLD YOU AND THE LAST TIME
6 - JOE THE MYNAH BIRD
7 - JOHN LENNON AND BRIAN KEITH
8 - CAN YOU PLEASE CRAWL OUT YOUR WINDOW?
9 - DOWNTOWN SHARON'S COLORFUL CHARACTERS
10 - WHATEVER HAPPENS FRANKIE.... DON'T RUN
11 - THE SATURDAY TRAIN TO YOUNGSTOWN
12 - SOUNDS LIKE A TRIP TO THE PENITENTIARY TO ME
13 - THE PERILS OF GROWING YOUR HAIR LONG 1966-68 AND BEYOND
14 - LIFE WAS GRAND IN THE SUMMER OF 1966
15 - THE LUNCH TABLE WELCOME
16 - BARBIE HYDE'S PARTY - OUR FIRST PROFESSIONAL GIG 1966
17 - JIM KENDZOR IN THE BAND
18 - LIGHT BULB HEAD AND MADRAS MAN
19 - THE LOCAL SCENE OF 1965-1968 - THE BANDS
20 - THE LOCAL SCENE OF 1966-1968 - THE VENUES
21 - 1967 - THE TIME OF TROUBLE STARTS
22 - MR. MARKS AND THE EPIPHONE CASINO
23 - THE BATTLE OF THE BANDS
24 - ST. JOE'S CAROUSEL TEEN CLUBS
25 - MR. BELVEDERE - GEOFF JONES
26 - STIV BATORS - 1969
27 - THE GREEN MAN, RAY ROBINSON
28 - A TRIP TO THE PSYCHEDELIC GAS STATION AND THE ELECTRIC ZOO - 1968
29 - ANYONE HAVE A MARLBORO?
30 - MY MOM AND DAD - A PAIR THAT WOULD BEAT A FULL HOUSE ANYTIME
31 - 1969's OK
32 - BIRTH OF BLUE ASH
33 - PARTY AT GOOG'S PAD (EVERY NIGHT)
34 - DAVID EVANS - EVAN HANLEY
35 - CHUCK BERRY - CLEVELAND PUBLIC HALL MARCH 26 - 1970
36 - WHENEVER YOU'RE TIRED OF BEING IN A CLOWN BAND
37 - SUMMER SOUL SPECTACULAR - 1970
38 - TOMMY
39 - BILL "CUPID" BARTOLIN JOINS BLUE ASH - 1970
40 - TINY TIM AND THE SHAH OF IRAN'S LIMOUSINE
41 - THE GREAT BOB MACK AND PITTSBURGH
42 - PEPPERMINT AND MERCURY
43 - CUPID'S BACHELOR PARTY AND A DARK HAIRED GIRL IN PICCADILLY CIRCUS
44 - RECORDING "NO MORE NO LESS" AT PEPPERMINT FEBRUARY, MARCH 1973
45 - ALMOST FAMOUS THE FIRST TIME - 1973
46 - SUNGLASS CITY
47 - OUR 2ND SINGLE RELEASE - JULY 1973
48 - YOKO ONO - OCTOBER 1973
49 - RASPBERRIES AND BLUE ASH - PACKARD MUSIC HALL - JANUARY 31 1974
50 - METALLIC KO AT THE MICHIGAN PALACE - FEBRUARY 9 1974
51 - THE JOINT IN THE WOODS AND AMERICAN BANDSTAND
52 - MERCURY POISONING....
53 - MEETING LISA IN BUHL PARK - JULY 3 1974
54 - CRAZY ASS
55 - PRINCE CARLTON, PRINCE TRACTION AND PRINCE DUDE
56 - ROCKIN AT THE MOCCASIN BAR

57 - PLAYBOY TIME
58 - MY HONEYMOON WITH THE DEAD BOYS - OCTOBER 1977
59 - ALMOST FAMOUS THE SECOND TIME (OVERVIEW 1979-81) STIV BATORS TO THE RESCUE
60 - TERRY HARTMAN - THE MAN WITH THE X-RAY EYES
61 - STIV BATORS BAND - THE DEAD BOYS TOURS AND THE ADVENTURES OF 1979-81
62 - JOHNNY BLITZ AND HIS FABULOUS DEAD BOYS
63 - NATIONAL RECORD MART #39
64 - 9:25 AND SEVEN SECONDS, WONDROUS STRANGE
65 - CLUB WOW, JIMMY ZERO - 1982 - 1985
66 - JACOB GEOFFREY SECICH
67 - I'VE BEEN AWAY 1990-2003
68 - MARK HERSHBERGER, AROUND AGAIN AND POP DETECTIVE
69 - DEADBEAT POETS - A NEW BEGINNING
70 - BLUE ASH REUNIONS AND REISSUES 2003 - 2009
71 - ON THE ROAD WITH THE DEADBEAT POETS - 2008
72 - CIRCUSTOWN
73 - COOLEST SONG IN THE WORLD - JULY 12 2010
74 - YOUNGSTOWN VORTEX SUTRA (THE BRITISH VERSION)
75 - EUROPEAN TOUR 2012
76 - JOHNNY SINCERE - HALLELUJAH ANYWAY 2013-2014 AND STRANGE TALES

1

ED SULLIVAN.. THAT BASTARD RUINED EVERYTHING!

One day in 1970 or 1971 my dad, Frank and I were watching the Ed Sullivan Show. My dad started shaking his head slowly and said to me 'Ed Sullivan.. That bastard ruined everything!' About once every 5 years my dad would blurt out something very funny and profound. More on his views on religion and politics later in this book. The more I think of it my dad's world was headed to ruin on February 9, 1964 when the Beatles first appeared on The Ed Sullivan Show. I remember it as clear as day watching the show with my sisters, Cindy and Maryann and my mom and dad. My dad would start up for the TV teasing us 'Let's see what's on over at ABC' and we'd scream, 'No, no don't change the channel'. 'Maybe something good on NBC' and on and on as we watched transfixed at the black and white Philco.

I remember hearing the Beatles blasting through the loudspeakers while ice skating at Buhl Park on Lake Julia in Sharon, PA in early January of 1964. *I Want To Hold Your Hand* as all over the radio waves by then as well but actually seeing the Beatles and the mania on TV fundamentally did change everyone's world that night. I know it did mine. My life as a star baseball player, an honor student and all around good Catholic boy would soon to be in shambles. Now, all I wanted to do was be in a band. The only really cool thing that I'd done in my 12 years of so far then was shake Senator John Kennedy's hand when he came to our town of Sharon, PA in October of 1960.

I remember the day after (Monday, February 10th) the Beatles appeared on Ed Sullivan going to school and looking out from the 3rd floor window of my 7th grade home room in the adjacent Annex building into Sharon Junior High School and Principal Pete Collodi's 2nd floor office. About half a dozen of the upperclassmen hoods (Ray Popa included) were being sent home from school. Overnight they had taken the grease out of their hair and had Beatle-like long hair that was even longer than the Beatles. Ray's mom was a hairdresser so she must have done it. They all soon went back to the Brylcream and Wild Root DA's but I slowly started growing mine forever more that day. The British Invasion had infested the halls of Sharon Junior High School just 12 hours after it breached the walls of America.

I started playing harmonica because a lot of the early Beatles songs employed it and I got pretty good at it. I also started tinkering with an old Stella guitar that my Uncle Jack had given me. I became obsessed with music. I listened to all the great AM stations I could get at the time WHOT in Youngstown with the legendary Boots Bell, WKYC in Cleveland and CKLW in Windsor, Ontario. If I wasn't listening to radio, I'd be playing or trading records with my neighborhood friends Gayle Holland, Beaver Warner, Jimmy Disko, Lynne Richter, Lianne Haney, Mary Jo Chizmar and Nicky Rock. We all loved this new music from England. My best friend, Mark 'Beaver' Warner lived on Haig St. a few houses east of the Chizmars. Beaver had a Kay electric guitar and already knew some chords and riffs and started to teach me. My mom, Dolly bought me my first playable guitar which was a Harmony Monterrey sunburst acoustic with f-holes for $75.00 which was a lot of money back then.

Another big influence on me was Ray Chizmar (Mary Jo's older brother) who had a first-rate local band called 'Mickey Farrell and The Dynamics' and before that the 'The Fairlanes' with the DePretas and Mickey Farrell. We'd often watch them rehearse in Chizmar's basement. Ray was the first really cool person I had ever met. He was Bobby Darin, Buddy Holly and Edd 'Kookie' Byrnes all rolled into one. When I'd see him when I was a kid I'd say 'What do ya say, Ray?' And he'd say 'Whatcha got in the bank, Frank?'. He was a real cool cat. Mickey Farrell and The Dynamics actually made records. *Wong Foo* in 1963 and *Baby Mine* in 1964 on the Bethlehem label both of which are highly valued collector's items today. To this day they are still played on WFMU one of the coolest stations in the country in the New York/New Jersey area. Ray played guitar and wrote the songs. We used to think they were so cool. Beaver and I idolized Ray. We had a real Rock 'n' Roll Star in our own neighborhood. When Ray went in the Air Force he told us we could borrow his guitars from his dad Chic if we had any big gigs. We did a couple of times and treated those Gibson and Epiphone guitars like gold. We'd bring them back with new strings and polished and shined. We were so grateful as we had such crummy equipment. Ray tragically died in an automobile accident on an icy highway in late December 1968. He was only 24 years old.

When the Beatles landed here and it was all over but the shouting for me so to speak. I was primed and ready to go. I knew what I wanted to do with my life. Throughout the rest of 1964 and 1965 all I wanted to do was be in a band but I had to learn to play first. Beaver and I would practice guitar every day. His dad Fran played guitar a little too and taught us some country songs and by the spring of 1965 we started playing for the neighborhood kids and had formed our first band the Electrons. We'd do our best to learn songs by slowing down the records and by looking at sheet music in the music stores but they always had the wrong key from the records. One of the best things we did was to start to write our own songs. My first was *Let Me Go* a poor attempt to copy the Kinks *Set Me Free* and Beaver's first was *Run And Dance In*

The Meadow which was actually a pretty good song which we would do 'live' and in person. Two others I remember that we wrote together back then were *He Was Poor* which wasn't bad and *Happy Maria* which was hilarious. In the years 1964 and 1965 we were bombarded with great TV shows that seemed to be on almost every day: Shindig. Shivaree, Hullabaloo, Hollywood A Go-Go, Where The Action Is, The Ed Sullivan Show, Hollywood Palace and American Bandstand that would all feature the latest British Invasion, Motown, West Coast Folk Rock and Soul Sounds. I'd carry around photos of the Kinks, Rolling Stones and also Beatles trading cards in my wallet (which I still do). What I'll be telling in this book is how it was a great time to be alive, loving this new music, falling in love for the first time and the second time, meeting and knowing some very colorful characters in my life, having more laughs than any man should ever have the right to and growing up and getting kicks and getting old in a small provincial working-class town called Sharon, Pennsylvania 'The Friendly City' (pop. 26,267 in 1966) on the Ohio border.

2

GOD HAS A TREMENDOUS SENSE OF HUMOR

My family lived on March Street two blocks from Farrell, PA. My father, Frank was a steelworker at Sharon Steel and a World War II Army veteran who served in the South Pacific and my mom, Dolly was a cake decorator at Metz Bakery which was around the corner from our house. She would later go into business for herself making wedding cakes and was quite successful at it. She also worked at Westinghouse making torpedoes during World War II. I have two sisters, Cindy who is 4 years older than me and Maryann who is two years younger. We all went to St. Anthony Of Padua Roman Catholic Church except for my dad. My paternal grandparents, Stephen and Mildred Secich (pronounced SESS-ich) were Croatian immigrants from the Austro-Hungarian Empire in the early 1900'S. as were my maternal grandparents John and Mary Abranovich who lived on a farm near Pulaski, PA. Most people in our town worked in steel mills like Sharon Steel and National Castings or factories like Westinghouse, Sawhill, GATX and the many others that were running full bore here in the 1960's. The big excitement would be the Sharon-Farrell high school rivalry in football and basketball every year, the annual Hoyle Basketball Tournament at the Buhl Club every spring and church and county fairs in the summer. Sharon is also unique in the fact that it has the only free golf course in the world, Buhl Farm Golf Course which is known as Dum Dum by us locals.

I attended St. Anthony's Catholic school (where I went to school with Carl Jaklic who would be become one of the best guitarists ever in the Shenango Valley and played in a great local band Buster Crab) from Grades 4-6 in 1960-63. Every year the carnival would come to town and set up behind the VFW a block east of the school on the other side of the rat-infested trash dump. All the Shenango Valley Catholic churches would annually have bazaars and picnics and fetes. Once when we were about 10 years old Beaver and I went to the church bazaar at St. Anthony's. We spent all afternoon playing games of chance but were having no luck.

We ended up at the ring toss booth where they'd have prizes like paper money wrapped around wooden stakes and you'd have put the ring around it. The closer, easier to ring wooden stakes had cheap prizes like Chinese straw finger cuffs and plastic kazoos. The money stakes were farther away. It was a hard game to win anything good. Beaver threw at a ring and it landed on a ten dollar bill. It was amazing. That was a fortune. I was down to my last dime and had only one ring left to throw so I shut my eyes and prayed to God to win. The furthest away wooden stake just had a note that said "**GRAND PRIZE ONLY ONE WINNER**".

I thought that has to be a twenty dollar bill or maybe even a fifty. I closed my eyes, threw it and prayed with all my might (made the I'll never be bad again, I promise prayer) and it landed on the Grand Prize. I couldn't believe it. Priests and nuns were coming from everywhere with noise makers and confetti and everyone gathered around and a big box was brought out. 'You've won the Grand Prize at this year's fair'. I opened it up and it was a statue of the Infant of Prague all bedecked and bejeweled in satin robes with fake gems and a gold painted-on crown. You should have seen the look on my face. You could have knocked me over with a feather. It was one of the great object lessons of my life and since then I have always considered myself a lucky person.

From that day forward I have believed in the workings of God and especially that he has a tremendous sense of humor..... Or at least he does with me. I took the IOP home and gave it to my mom, Dolly who was a devout Catholic and she thought the whole thing was a riot. 'Be careful for what you pray for as prayers can come true'. The truly weird thing that came from all this is that I became one the best carnival game players ever throughout my life. I have won my nieces and nephews and my son, Jake countless huge stuffed animals and hardly ever spent much money on it. At one point my wife, Lisa and I had to clear out our cellar that was full of big stuffed animals. It's one remarkably worthless and useless talent that I possess.

It's funny (he says skipping ahead 50 years to) one day in January of 2012 when my band the Deadbeat Poets were touring in Prague in the Czech Republic with New York Junk. Joe Sztabnik of NYJ and I took a walk one afternoon through the cobblestone streets of Prague to see the sights. We ended up walking past a high school where at street level we could look in the windows at the students paying attention to and taking notes from their instructor. All but for the exception of one kid with long blonde hair in a leather jacket who was sound asleep near a window in the back. Joe nudges me points to him and says 'Hey, Frank, there's me and you 45 years ago' and we just busted up laughing. Some things never change anywhere on this planet. On every street corner in Prague merchants sell a wide variety of the Infant Of Prague souvenirs along with Adolf Hitler masks and leftover Communist era hats complete with hammer and sickle badges. That day, I bought a mini Infant Of Prague for my Mom, Dolly for a souvenir and she got the greatest kick out of it as she always loved telling anyone of my Infant Of Prague carnival story. My mom was in a nursing home for the last four months of her life. She always kept that miniature Infant Of Prague on her night stand there. She passed away at the age of 91 on June 24, 2014.

3

REBELS WITHOUT A PAUSE

Back then in the 60's as budding teenagers we'd also do a lot of things for laughs and our own amusement. Some of our favorite pastimes were throwing snowballs at cars, knocking on doors and running, having dirt bomb fights, shooting rats with BB guns, arrows and sling shots at the dump by the school, blowing up garbage cans with M80's and Cherry Bombs with a cigarette time fuse (preferably a Pall Mall or Chesterfield King or a king-sized York that had no filter) where you'd stick the M80 or Cherry Bomb stiff green fuse in the unlit end, then the cigarette would slowly burn down until it lit the fuse. It would take about 15 minutes so you could be far away from the scene of the crime when the fire cracker went off or be innocently standing by. It was a great ploy at dances, at school, football games, whenever there were police around or for leaving on someone's front porch or in their trash can. Smashing pumpkins and soaping windows were done in the fall. Bumper dragging or hanging on a bumper of a moving car on icy or snowy roads was also great fun but could be dangerous at times. All in all we were pretty harmless and just punks with attitudes.

We'd also crawl in the sewers of the city. One particularly good place was right where Route 62 meets Stambaugh Avenue near the old fire station. The one good way to get in the Sharon City sewer system was to scale a practically 15 foot vertical wall where the creek waterfalled by the fire station. Then you'd enter an area where you could sit and look out through a 3ft. long and 6 inches high opening on the street where water could run off into the sewers. It was perfect because cars had to stop at a red light there. We would tap underneath the car with a stick or tap the hubcaps and the drivers would get out and look around trying to find the noise. When they got back in we'd do it again. Sometimes we'd yell insults at the people in the cars especially if it was good weather and they never knew where it came from. We'd yell 'Up in the tree you hillbilly asshole' and they would swear and crane their necks out the window to look.

4

FREE BEER!

Another one of the great pastimes in our neighborhood other than playing and listening to music was stealing cases of beer from the neighborhood drive-thru beer stores which were and are peculiar to Western, PA and Northeast Ohio where a customer would drive their car through, open the trunk and a case beer would be ordered, paid for and loaded in the car trunk all in one fell swoop. When the stream of cars going through the Drive-Thru would trickle to nothing. A couple of us would watch from the front area where the owners and workers were and a few of us would go up to the back and grab a couple cases of Iron City Beer and bolt with it. Ray Popa, who I have previously mentioned was a legendary character in this endeavor. He actually stole a case of beer while on crutches and with a broken leg which looms large in Sharon teenage JD folklore. The beer distributor did such a volume business that I don't think they ever missed the occasional case or two. In winter time we would hide the beer in a little shed that my dad had built in our back yard. He kept the lawn mower there and other yard tools and never went in there in the winter.

One Winter's day my father burst in through the back door of our house where Ray, Nicky Rock and me were sitting. He goes 'You guys will never believe this, I just found 3 cases of Iron City beer in my shed.. God Damn did I ever get struck lucky', why don't you guys give me a hand and help bring it in?'. We couldn't believe it. He busted us without saying, confiscated our beer, made us do the manual labor and there was nothing we could do about it.

5

EIGHT ARMS TO HOLD YOU AND THE LAST TIME

Musically speaking in 1964 and into 1965 much of mine and my friends lives revolved around the Beatles and the Rolling Stones. I couldn't even count the number of times I saw 'A Hard Day's Night' in the summer and fall of 1964. Back then you could buy one ticket and stay all day for all the showings. Beaver Warner, Jimmy Disko and I did that uncountable times. Beatles '65 had just come out and I got one for Christmas of 1964 and I played it incessantly during that winter. One time my mom and dad had to go to a wedding reception and my sisters were elsewhere and I had the house to myself. Once my parents left after I gave them assurances for the fifth time that I'd be alright and wouldn't burn the house down, I got out my Beatles '65 album and started singing along with *No Reply, I'm A Loser* and then *Baby's In Black* but when it came to *Rock And Roll Music* I cranked it full blast on our stereo console so that the walls were shaking. I was singing with a pretend microphone and then screaming it John Lennon style writhing and rolling on the floor and shrieking like a mad man, all of a sudden I looked over and in the doorway there were my Mom and Dad (speechless with the most incredulous looks I'd ever seen on their faces). Quite embarrassed, I scurried over to the stereo to turn it down. There was an awkward silence for a moment then my Dad (who normally in this kind of situation would not be a calm man) calmly said 'we forgot the wedding card'. He took the envelope from on top of the TV and they left and no one ever said another word about it. My Rock 'n' Roll career had begun. Johnny Sincere was born.

As the best year for music ever in my opinion 1965 opened, I was by now a hopeless case and immersed in this incredible new music. The Beatles had killer #1 singles in a row *I Feel Fine, Eight Days A Week* and *Ticket To Ride* with the subtitle from the United Artists release 'Eight Arms To Hold You' which was later changed to 'Help!'

Other Number One's were: *You've Lost That Lovin' Feeling, Stop In The Name Of Love, Mr. Tambourine Man, Yesterday, Get Off Of My Cloud, (I Can't Get No) Satisfaction, Hang On Sloopy, Over And Over, I Got You Babe, My Girl, Eve Of Destruction, Help Me Rhonda, This Diamond Ring, I Hear A Symphony, Downtown, I Can't Help Myself, Help!*.

The Number One songs in Billboard Magazine for these weeks in a row in 1965 were all from British bands:

April 10	*I'm Telling You Now*	- Freddie And The Dreamers
April 17	*I'm Telling You Now*	- Freddie And The Dreamers
April 24	*Game Of Love*	- Wayne Fontana & The Mindbenders
May 01	*Mrs. Brown You've Got A Lovely Daughter*	- Herman's Hermits
May 08	*Mrs. Brown You've Got A Lovely Daughter*	- Herman's Hermits

The bands were not only all British but they were all from the same city of Manchester.

The following songs made Billboard's Top 5 in 1965.

Love Potion # 9
The Name Game
King Of The Road
Shotgun
I'll Never Find Another You
Wooly Bully
Wonderful World
Can't You Hear My Heartbeat
Silhouettes
Cara Mia
Henry The VIII
What's New Pussycat?
Yes, I'm Ready
California Girls
Like A Rolling Stone
Unchained Melody
You Were On My Mind
Catch Us If You Can
Treat Her Right
The In Crowd
A Lover's Concerto
Keep On Dancing
Everybody Loves A Clown
1-2-3
You're The One
Rescue Me
Let's Hang On
I Got You (I Feel Good)
The Sound Of Silence

I could list the songs the made the Top 40 in 1965 but you'd stare in disbelief. I could list the songs that cracked the Top 100 in 1965 and your head would explode. Look it up sometime. It is astounding the output of great music in the year 1965. It's truly unequaled in musical history.

One day, in the spring of 1965, I was in my family's car on Wallis Ave. While my mom shopped in G. C. Murphy's 5 & 10 in Farrell, I turned the radio dial to 1470 WFAR. That's where I first heard the opening Brian Jones riff that starts the Rolling Stones legendary song *The Last Time*. It literally shook my world so much so that every time I have heard it since, I get the same reaction of coolness and the hairs on my arms and neck stand up and I stop and listen like it was the National Anthem.

JOHNNY SINCERE

(Frank Secich)

Ladies & gentlemen
The face of 1963...Mr. Johnny Sincere!
I'm singing "3 Cute Chicks"
They all love me here
Man, I can take my pick
I really like the blonde who looks just like
Right out of 1956

Meet Mr. Sammy Rivers, my friend & piano man
He knows some crazy chords
Lays down some pertinent jams
While I juggle the words
Never ever using my hands

Oh Johnny, in a world of lonely hearts out there (go Johnny go, go Johnny go)
For Johnny, you know, you know no one will shed a tear (No one will shed a tear)
No Johnny, No No Not for Johnny Sincere

I used to work in a place
In an office like that
Selling policies for some big fat cat
No, It wasn't very cool, So, I got out of that

When my girl is all alone
She plays a wicked Sousaphone
Even floating in the water
She weighs some 17 stone
Yet, she's a positive & level headed girl
Who swings like a saxophone

Mr. Gilmour had an ice pick in the electrical lab
He put on a white coat & then he started to stab
Wildly at the speakers & as I was calling a cab

Put on my rock & roll sneakers
They were Red Ball Jets
Black & white as I recall.... maybe I forget
When the taxi came & went
They were soaking wet

6

JOE THE MYNAH BIRD

Okay, I know let's get to the musical inspirations. Back in the 1960's there was a department store in the Hickory Plaza in Sharon called S.S. Kresge which later became Kmart. They had a small pet section with tropical fish, lizards, turtles and a talking Mynah bird named Joe. Joe was classic. He only knew dirty words that were taught to him by Beaver Warner, Jimmy Disko, myself and others. Joe's vocabulary was legendary in the Shenango Valley and of course I wrote a song about him as performed and recorded by the Deadbeat Poets and released in Spain in 2015 on Kick Out The Jams Records.

JOE THE MYNAH BIRD

(Frank Secich)

Let's go see Joe the mynah bird
Find out what new words he's learned
No one would take home Joe it's sad
Because his language was so bad

Us kids would teach Joe dirty words
Then fall about when he conferred
Laugh until our sides would split
Every time Joe'd let it rip

Joe the Mynah Bird
Dropping F-bombs on grandmother
Joe The Mynah Bird
Funniest thing you ever heard

The S.S. Kresge's employees
Tried to teach that mocking bird to sing
All their efforts went for naught
As Joe rained down profanity

The serious customers complained
About the bad bird every day
They'd repeat the same refrain
While expecting things to change

Then one day no more Joe
Our beloved bird was gone (quite ominously)
The department store has Musak now
That blends into the wall (quite colorlessly)
But if you listen hard enough
You can hear him call

Someone bought him renamed him Jack
Very next day they brought him back
Those who worked there used to say
They could not give Joe away

He kept our small minds entertained
Time well spent in reverie
Joe could not hide his disdain
For those who were outside his cage

Joe The Mynah Bird
Dropping F-bombs on priests and nuns

Joe The Mynah Bird
Wildest thing you ever heard
Craziest thing you ever head
Funniest thing you ever heard

But if you listen hard enough
You can hear him call

7

JOHN LENNON AND BRIAN KEITH

My hair was as long as John Lennon's that summer but I had to get it cut as part of my punishment for running away from home. This was August of 1965. There was some trouble at the time so me and my friend, Jack Reilly ran away. We eluded the authorities in Hubbard & Chestnut Ridge & ended up on Belmont Ave. in Youngstown around midnight. We were headed for Australia. After resting on the lawn chairs by the pool of the Holiday Inn about 1:00 am we started hitching on Belmont and a station wagon pulled over about where Denny's Restaurant is now. Driver: 'Where are you headed boys?', Me: 'Sydney, Australia', Driver: 'Jesus Christ, that's as about as god damned far as you can get from Youngstown', Me: 'Exactly', Driver; 'Well, get in, are you guys runaways or something?', Me: 'Yeah, we are'. Driver: 'Okay, I have a buddy who's a truck driver and he's headed to Cincinnati in a few hours and I'm sure he'll let you tag along', Me: 'How cool'. So, he drives over to this bar on Albert St. (of all places) to find his friend. Meanwhile, we're sitting in his car while he supposedly goes to get his buddy. Then two ladies came out to the car to talk to us and then the guy also comes out. All of a sudden a Youngstown squad car pulls up with two cops. Turns out he was a nice guy and had ratted us out. So, we're in the cop car and the first policeman says, 'Okay, who are you boys?' 'What are your names?' Me: 'I'm, John Lennon' then Jack says, 'I'm Brian Keith'. Then the second policeman: 'Well, well, what have we got here? A Beatle and an actor'. So they took us to the police station but we wouldn't say a thing.

When we were alone I asked Jack, 'Why did you say Brian Keith?' Jack said, 'That's my favorite actor and my two favorite Stones'. They did feed us and I have to admit that the food there was pretty good. After a couple of hours a police Sgt. came in and asked, 'Alright, which one of you is Jack?' Jack said, 'That would be me'. Then the officer said, 'Well I wouldn't want to be you. I just talked to your old man and he's on his way over'. I started laughing and the cop said, 'I wouldn't laugh so hard, Mr. Secich, your father is up in Cleveland looking for you guys and he's even more pissed than Jack's dad'. You can guess the rest. Years later, I told this story to Anita Pallenberg and she howled. She said, 'I'm going to tell this story to Keith, he'll love it'.

After being grounded for a couple of weeks for my first outing I went to see the Dave

Clark Five movie 'Having A Wild Weekend' with my sister Cindy (who was a big fan of theirs) at the Columbia Theater in Sharon sporting a short haircut.

8

CAN YOU PLEASE CRAWL OUT YOUR WINDOW?

I went to my first proper concert on November 12, 1965 at Cleveland Music Hall. It was Bob Dylan on his famous first electric tour. I took a small suitcase to school and after school my friends Nick Rock, Doreen (Brooks) Clark, Linda Pollock walked me over to the Continental Trailways station on S. Main Avenue in Sharon. I travelled 100 miles on the bus and arrived at Chester station in Cleveland about 6:30 pm. I met my older sister, Cindy (who was going to nursing school) in Cleveland and her friend Ellen. They dropped me off at the concert. I had no idea of the earth-shaking, eye-opening, mind-blowing experience that was about to happen to me and change my life forever. It is still the best concert that I have ever seen or heard. There was no opening act. Dylan opened with a folk set and then the full out band. The backing band was the Hawks (The Band) but with another drummer not Levon Helm. Dylan was one of the first performers ever to travel with a great sound system. My ticket was in the balcony right in the middle in the first row. There were no boos from the Cleveland fans that night. I heard Dylan later say that Cleveland and Minneapolis were the only places they didn't get boos on that infamous 1965-66 world tour.

The acoustic set was spellbinding enough, *Mr. Tambourine Man, It's All Over Now, Baby Blue, Desolation Row, To Ramona, She Belongs To Me* and so many other great ones from that period but the electric set hit me like an atomic bomb, *Like A Rolling Stone, Tombstone Blues, Highway 61 Revisited, Queen Jane Approximately, Subterranean Homesick Blues* and an electric version of *It Ain't Me Babe*. But the transcendent moment for me was when Bob got on the grand piano for *Positively 4th Street* and *Ballad Of A Thin Man*. After the concert Cindy and Ellen picked me up and I stayed the weekend at their student dormitory.

The next morning was a Saturday and I took the bus from their dormitory to downtown Cleveland to buy records at the famed Record Rendezvous. I bought the one Dylan album I didn't have *Freewheelin' Bob Dylan* and three singles *Get Off Of My Cloud, Colours* and *Do You Believe In Magic?* I still have the Dylan LP and the Donovan and Stones singles but the Lovin' Spoonful disc is long gone. My dad picked me up on Sunday and I went back to Sharon as a 14 year old on a mission. I no longer even had the slightest pretense about caring for schoolwork or my studies. Algebra and French didn't have anything to do with the Rolling Stones and the Animals as far as I was concerned. I would walk the streets of Sharon with my Lennon/Dylan leather cap and Monterrey strapped across my back and my harmonica holder hanging around my neck and play *Universal Soldier* or *It's All Over Now, Baby Blue* for anyone who would listen, Rosemary Yesko Gregory, Gwynne Allen...

One of the cool things back then is that my family would go to Canada at least twice a year to visit relatives in Hamilton and Welland, Ontario. It was really cool for me because you could get great records, magazines and clothes from England in Canada that you just couldn't get in America. So, I'd always save my money from my Pittsburgh Post-Gazette newspaper route, my Grit Newspaper route, TV Guide route and from selling popcorn for "Mike The Popcorn Man" at all the Farrell High games for those trips to Canada. There I would learn about bands like Scotland's, The Poets, The Creation, The Pretty Things, The Undertakers and The Merseybeats and even rarer British bands that not many in the States would know about.

9

DOWNTOWN SHARON'S COLORFUL CHARACTERS

We'd hang around a lot on Saturday afternoons in downtown Sharon where all the action was. We'd eat and hang out at the Coney Island hot dog shoppe or Sotus Grille and usually go to a matinee at the Columbia Theater for 35 cents. Downtown Sharon was then, is now and will be forever filled with colorful characters. We used to call them "Tractions". Howard Rawlia (known as Howie who was actually a distant relative by marriage to my wife, Lisa and I have never let her live it down) who always wore orange and black the (Sharon High colors) and sat court side or at the 50 yard line in front of every basketball or football game. The Indian who wore long hair braided like a native American but was really Hungarian. The Wolf Man, Oscar Bonner (a country singer who wore a Stetson and would always play guitar and sing on the corner on Main and West State St.), Pat (an affable old black man who would dress in an Army/Navy Store olive green trench coat and matching Russian hat and carry a snow shovel and always say "Stayin' in school?", The Leaner (who would just lean against available poles) and last but not least the legendary "Pop Bottle Jones's" and we'll get to them shortly.

There was also one particularly ill-tempered, curmudgeonly old gentleman who would always look at us and mumble "Long-Haired Sons A Bitches!......Get out the way!" Then take a wimpy swipe at us with his cane. After months of this kind of street theater one day we were on the Shenango River Bridge as he went to hit me with his cane, I'd had enough. I snatched his hat off his head and tossed it into the Shenango River. 'There you hatless old bastard, now you really have something to bitch about!' I guess we qualified as Downtown Sharon characters ourselves.

10

WHATEVER HAPPENS FRANKIE.... DON'T RUN

Okay, time to get back to the Pop Bottle Jones's. I would be remiss in my duties and have done a great disservice to the annals of Sharon's juvenile delinquents and oddball characters if I did not for the first time tell this story. The Pop Bottle Jones's were a family that lived on the West Hill of Sharon back then which borders the Ohio state line. The Jones's were a large family who were all very small and had high squeaky voices and they all looked remarkably the same. They would comb and canvass the town and the ditches off the highways for glass soda pop bottles which could be redeemed at that time for the deposit at any store. There was a 2 cent deposit for a small bottle and nickel for quart bottles. The Jones's would roam the streets with metal shopping carts and red wagons and scavenge pop bottles everywhere in town. It was how they made their living as people littered a lot back then. A couple of generations later they still exist in Sharon only now they have modernized with the times and collect aluminum cans. One time in early 1966 it must have been, Ray Popa and myself found ourselves having a cigarette on the street outside their house on the West Hill. Me being the apprentice hoodlum and Ray the journeyman.

It was already after dark. Ray bends down and picks up a small brickbat off the street and looks at me and says 'Whatever happens Frankie.... Don't Run!'. Suddenly, Ray fires a Bob Feller fastball brickbat right through one of their small windows. 'Don't run, Frankie!' I just froze in my tracks. A few seconds later one of the Jones's peeps out through another window at us. Ray calls him outside. He says 'Mr. Jones, a car full of drunken hoods just drove by throwing rocks at us and your house. Frankie and I were just standing here minding our own business. We couldn't believe it. Looked like Brookfield or Masury assholes. They sped right up the hill into Ohio. Then Ray says with all the balls in the world 'You want me to call the cops for you?' Mr. Jones says, 'Okay' So we go in their house to use the telephone. I'm just dying inside as this is so unbelievably funny. A few minutes later a squad car arrives. Talk about grace under pressure, Ray gives the police an eyewitness account. 'This car came around the corner with 3 or 4 hoods yelling and driving crazy. I think they may have been drunk. It was a white '61 Dodge with Ohio plates. I couldn't get the license number. It happened really fast then they sped up the street into Ohio'. The cops not caring much assessed the minor damage and took the report, thanked us and left. Walking home after we never laughed so hard

11

THE SATURDAY TRAIN TO YOUNGSTOWN

On Saturdays circa 1966-67 there was a train that ran daily from New York to Chicago and stopped in Sharon and Youngstown on the way, back then you could ride from Sharon to Youngstown for 59 cents. You could stay all day in the YO then take a bus or the train again back to Sharon in the evening. Some Saturdays we'd take quite a gang: Myself, Tim Hendrich, Mike Kiefer, Bill Rudge, Beaver Warner, Nicky Rock, Joe Cvelbar, Bob Lyshoir, Jack Reilly, Chuck Borawski, Rich Delacroix, Tony Nicastro, Fran Warner, Jim Kendzor and others. The first place we'd hit in Youngstown was the Strouss Music Store which was right near the train station and college on Wick Ave. They were the only Rickenbacker guitar retailer around and they'd have tons of Ricks and let you play them as much as you wanted. Then we'd hit the Hartzell, Rose and Son clothier where they had imported clothes from England, There was a Record Rendezvous or the "Voo" as it was known in Youngstown too. We'd also walk up Market Street to Dusi Music on the south side. One time, Fran Warner actually walked on his hands on the rail of the Market St. Bridge which spanned the Mahoning River. Fran was an amazing athlete and gymnast as part of the Buhl Club Whiz Kids who appeared on the Ted Mack Show and so was Billy Rudge. We'd also hit the Salvation Army and Goodwill stores downtown. We'd buy old Zoot Suits and double-breasted suits from the 1940's and cast off World War Two uniforms for 25 or 50 cents. We'd also buy used marching band uniforms and this was before Sgt. Pepper. We'd always make quite a day of it and would return at night with our loot on the train or the bus.

12

SOUNDS LIKE A TRIP TO THE PENITENTIARY TO ME

On many a cold morning my friend, Clifford would pull his coat collar up around his ears and steam out these words 'You know this is fucked up, Secich. Walking to school when it's 10 degrees below zero, at 7:30 in the morning up and down these hills, so that we can maybe get through high school and be lucky enough to get a job in one of these steel mills and work our asses off for the rest of our lives. It's fucked up. We should quit and join up with my cousin Elvin in Akron'.

Then he'd lighten up and regale me with tales of his Ohio cousin, Elvin Dabney. 'Elvin is a professional thief, man, He's got tons of money and chicks and cars like you wouldn't believe. He even has 'Elvin Dabney Professional Thief' printed on his business card.' I said 'I don't know Clifford, sounds like a trip to the penitentiary to me'. 'Nah man, Elvin is too slick and too smart. The cops could never catch him. He steals shit made to order. You want a Lincoln Continental he'll get it, a diamond ring for your engaged lady he'll get it for you at a reduced rate and his share is all profit. The Dude is a genius. He's known all over the world, man: Akron, Canton, Cleveland, Detroit, Youngstown, Pittsburgh............ Buffalo!

ELVIN DABNEY PROFESSIONAL THIEF

(Frank Secich)

Elvin Dabney Professional Thief
That's what his business card reads
"Known all over the world"
Always with a beautiful girl

Elvin came from Akron town
In a place they call North Howard Street
With it's pool halls and it's gay bars &
Storefront Baptist churches trying save them all

My friends and I, we idolized him
We wanted to be just like him
To steal like the rich
And give to ourselves
Always carry a wad and wear shit-eating grin, like

Elvin Dabney Professional Thief
That's what his business card reads
"Known all over the world"
Always with a beautiful girl

Law enforcement knew all about it
But could never bring charges on him
He was just too slick just too smart
They couldn't nab Elvin in a million years

The authorities tried to set him up
But he was always way too smart
The more that they would harass him
He would just embarrass them
One day Elvin up and left
Took all his loot away he went
Some folks say to Panama
But nobody was really sure at all

About Elvin Dabney Professional Thief

Strange but true the tales were tall
We heard Elvin had invested it all
A model citizen legitimate and all
Donating checks at the charity ball

That he was living down south like a king
In the lap of luxury
In church every Sunday
To bow down give thanks
He's off to vacation summers
In the Outer Banks

That's Elvin Dabney Professional Thief

Known all over the world
Akron, Canton, Cleveland, Detroit
Youngstown, Pittsburgh......Buffalo!

13

THE PERILS OF GROWING YOUR HAIR LONG 1966-68 AND BEYOND

In the first week of June of 1966, Beaver Warner and myself had to take an English class (which we had flunked in Junior High) over again in summer school at Sharon Senior High School in order to pass from the 9th to the 10th grade. The first day of summer school we walked into class and sat down. I sat right in front of the teacher's desk. She was in her early twenties with short blonde hair and one would have found her attractive at first sight. She was leaning back half-sitting on her desk and just kept staring at me as the class took their seats. She just kept staring until the class got quiet then she started slowly shaking her head. So, finally I said 'Is there a problem?' To which she snakily replied 'I was just wondering, if you were a boy or if you were a girl?' (A little nervous laughter from the class). Then I said, with perfect comic timing 'That's so funny,because I was just wondering the exact same thing about YOU!' (Uproarious laughter from the class).

She screamed at me, 'HOW DARE YOU! HOW DARE YOU!' You go to Mr. Paxton's (the assistant principal's) office right now. Then Beaver got up and said 'You know you started it, lady but couldn't take it when Frank put you in your fuckin' place'. She then lost all control as if she hadn't already. 'YOU'RE OUT OF HERE TOO, MISTER!' She screamed at the Beaver. So we headed to the assistant principal's office laughing like hyenas. This was the first time we'd met Mr. Paxton. We told him what had happened. 'Where did you boys come from with that hair? What school did you go to?' I answered 'Sharon Junior High' and 'Mr. Collodi put up with those hairdos'. 'Yeah, he thinks it's cool. He's a big Stones fan'. 'Well, you can't go to Sharon High School unless you cut your hair'. We refused to cut our hair and were thrown out of summer school and had to repeat ninth grade.

We asked for our summer school tuition back that we had just paid in cash 30 minutes previously and we went out to celebrate. We never told our parents until the end of summer and then had to repeat Grade 9 in the Autumn which we fondly called 9-2. That's where we met Jim Kendzor on the first day of school so it was a good career move. Also, as an interesting side note is that years later I would buy the house next door to Mr. Paxton and we became pals.

14

LIFE WAS GRAND IN THE SUMMER OF 1966

I'm a strong believer that nothing is coincidence and everything is fate. I met both of the women that I fell in love with in my life at the same exact spot only eight years apart. In May of 1966, I was running from Freddie and Barney the park rangers in Buhl Park. I was soaking wet from swimming in one of the lakes with some of my friends which was forbidden. We scattered when the park police showed up. As I was running out of the park by the ball field toward Carley Avenue, I came across a very pretty girl that I had never seen before. Soaking dripping wet, I stopped and said 'Hello' then realizing they were in hot pursuit kept running. A few weeks later it was near the end of the school year and Sharon Junior High School would have a thing they called Recognition Day where the whole school would assemble in our assembly theater and principals and teachers would call the names of all the people who should receive recognition for their outstanding scholastic achievements and activities for the year and talented students performed and so on. This would take all morning: '9th grade cheerleaders please stand up', 'let's have a big hand for the Kegler's Club', a huge round of applause for the Girl's Tri-Hi-Y (and they'd always read the individual names) this went on for hundreds of such accolades. I was sitting at the very end of a row in the school theater with my friend, Dale Satterwhite and we would stand and take a bow, wave to the crowd for every activity even though we had participated in none of them. There were too many kids to seat in the hall so a lot of winners and performers just stood in the aisles next to the seats. Every time I made a funny remark, I could hear a girl's laughter from behind me. I turned around and it was her, the very girl I saw a few weeks before. Then at the end, Mr. Sample who was assistant principal and master of ceremonies that day said 'Now last and least let's give a big hand to the class clowns, Frank Secich and Dale Satterwhite'.

Then we disassembled and went to lunch and then our afternoon classes. I asked Beaver during lunch period if he noticed the girl who was standing next to me at the awards assembly? He said 'Yeah, her name is Mary Jean Hurlbert and she's a friend of Barbs' (Barbie Hyde was Beaver's girlfriend at the time). 'Could you tell her I'd like to meet her after school?' So, Beaver introduced me to Mary Jean after school by the flagpole and I walked her home. Mary Jean was a pretty blonde and attractively built. She was a cross between Marianne Faithfull and Mary Weiss of the Shangri-Las.

As we walked up East State St. I found that she had a great personality and a sense of humor and more importantly loved all the same records and bands I did. The Beatles, Stones, Kinks, Yardbirds, etc. By the end of walking her home and getting to know her on the couple of miles to Carley Ave, I was in love for the first time in my life.

That summer was magic. We'd all sit around the juke box at Buhl Farm Casino where we wore out two copies of *Paperback Writer* b/w *Rain* that summer or played *I Am A Rock* to death at Bello's Pizza. The Buhl Farm Casino Juke Box blasted *Hanky Panky* by Tommy James and the Shondells who were discovered by the great Bob Mack who I would have the immense pleasure to work with in another 4 years, *My Little Red Book* by Love, *Paint It Black* and *Mother's Little Helper* by the Stones, *Eight Miles High* by the Byrds, *Wild Thing* by the Troggs, *Little Red Riding Hood* by Sam The Sham and the Pharaohs, *Red Rubber Ball* by the Cyrkle, *When A Man Loves A Woman* by Percy Sledge and so many others.

A lot of the time we'd all sit on Hurlbert's back porch on lawn chairs and chain smoke Winston cigarettes and play records on a portable player or just talk and talk for hours (me, Mary Jean, Beaver Warner, Barbie Hyde, Rita May, Lee Ann Murphy, Jack Reilly, Gail Goldberg, Jane Davis and sometimes Connie Allum and Chuck Borawski) the whole gang of us. Those girls were all smart, good looking, witty and fun. Sometimes, I'd borrow the keys to Jane's mom's car (that Jane would hand over reluctantly) when her mother wasn't home and go joyriding. I had just turned 15 and wasn't old enough to drive. At times when there weren't many people there, Mary Jean and I would steal away any time we could to make out and be alone. That summer we spent a lot of time together. There were a lot of things to do. The Westinghouse Day Summer Picnic at Conneaut Lake Amusement Park, the Summer festival at St. Joe's, waterskiing on Conneaut Lake. Hanging out in our beautiful Buhl Park. If we were at Hurlbert's which we were a lot at 9:45pm on the dot just like clockwork Mary Jean's mom, Pat, would say through the kitchen window 'Mary Jean, It's about that time'. Then we'd all split to be home before curfew. In the fall we'd go to football games under the Friday Night lights (I can still smell the cigar smoke and taste the cold pizza) and after football season we'd take the bus on Friday nights to Greenville to go ice skating and make out on the bus ride home.

A lot of those girls, Barb, Rita, Jane, Gail, Debbie Kemp and Lil Swanson have remained great friends until this day and still get together at least once a year even though they live all over the country. I think that's so great they have that bond of friendship. They call themselves the Soul Sisters. I like that. So many of my old friends have passed on: Beaver Warner, Fran Warner, Chuck Borawski, Nick Rock, Ray Chizmar, Geoff Jones, Stiv Bators, Ray Popa, Paul Nelson and Bill Bartolin. The only way I can get back together with them is through my memories.

15

THE LUNCH TABLE WELCOME

Repeating 9th grade on the first day at school September, 1966 at Sharon Junior High School I first met Jim Kendzor. I had never seen him before because he had just transferred from Catholic school to public school. He had long blonde hair in the Brian Jones fashion. There were maybe ten kids at our school who had longer hair or if they didn't they were certified juvenile delinquents and misfits like me, Beaver, Joe Cvelbar, Rich Delacroix, Lou Myers, John Bosnjak, Jack Reilly, Bob Lyshoir. He came and sat down at our criminals table at lunchtime in the cafeteria. I think, Rich introduced me to Jim. I said to him 'Can you whip, Rich?' (Pointing at Rich). He said 'What?' I said 'Can you whip Rich.... In a fight?' He said 'I don't know' and I said 'Well, if you can't whip Rich then you can't whip me'.

Anyway, you look like Brian Jones so you've gotta be fairly cool so welcome to the table. We then started talking about music and I told him about our band. Jim said 'What's the name of your band?' I said 'We're the 'City Jail', but sometimes we're known as Left Eye'. We became fast friends and a month or two later I invited him up to my parent's house to hear us rehearse.

16

BARBIE HYDE'S PARTY – OUR FIRST PROFESSIONAL GIG 1966

Mark "Beaver" Warner, Jack Reilly and myself made our very first professional musical gig in September of 1966. It was at a party in Barbie Hyde's basement in Sharon. There were tons of our fellow Junior High students there. We practiced pretty hard for a month beforehand as we had been slacking off all summer with Barbie and Mary Jean. We only had two guitars and Jack played tambourine but we could sing pretty good. We borrowed a really nice big Gibson amp from Joe at the Sharon Music Center to sing through so I don't think we sounded too bad. I can remember clearly some of the songs we did such as *A Well Respected Man* by the Kinks or *Norwegian Wood* by the Beatles, *Just A Little* by the Beau Brummels and for some reason I clearly recall doing a folk version *Try Too Hard* by the Dave Clark Five. I know we also must have done *The House Of The Rising Sun, Little Black Egg, Yesterday's Gone* the Turtles version of *It Ain't Me Babe* and *Gloria*.

All in all the kids seemed to like it and we got over the jitters of playing out for the very first time. To make matters even cooler Barb's dad paid us $40.00 for the evening and that was very generous and cool of him. We were now professionals. Right after that we set about to realign the band.

17

JIM KENDZOR IN THE BAND

We knew had to get other members in the group so we picked up Bruce Miller on drums, Bill Rudge on bass and after Bruce moved to Cleveland we got Jeff Rozniata on drums and added Scott Deans on third guitar....... And then we got Jim Kendzor. Jim is one of the great singers of Rock and Roll in my opinion. He can sing anything, has perfect pitch and has a very high range in natural voice like Little Richard, Robert Plant, Roger Daltrey, Eric Carmen, Steve Marriott, Noddy Holder or Paul McCartney. It's a real gift and very few possess it but don't tell him I said that because he'll get a big head. I can't ever remember him doing more than one take in a recording session. He was that good. Film Director Frank Capra used to say about Barbara Stanwyck that she was the perfect actress and never had to do a scene over again. Jim was like that.

When we were in 9th grade with the band we hadn't by any means risen to the professional level in our musical ability like say Phil Keaggy or Roger Lewis or the Doug Thomas and Gary McCoy of the Holes In The Road or Dick Belli or Ting Markulin of the Human Beinz but we could really sing and then with Jim we got much better. Around October 1966, I invited Jim up to my parent's house where we'd rehearse. I think the only reason he came was that he was interested in my sister, Maryann. Mind you, I still had never heard him sing yet. We ran through some of our best numbers *It's All Over Now, The Last Time, Do Wah Diddy Diddy* and others.

Earlier in school that day I had asked Jim if could sing. He said 'I'm not bad'. So at practice I asked him if he wanted to sing one. He said 'Okay, I'll try one'. I said 'How about *Long Tall Sally* in the same key as the Beatles (thinking he'll never do this as it's so hard to sing and we'll have a good laugh) so I cued him and counted 1..2..3.. and Jim went, 'I'm gonna tell Aunt Mary about Uncle John'............ all the way through nailing it as good as Paul McCartney or Little Richard ever did. We were floored. I learned the second great object lesson of my life. Never underestimate anyone. I looked at Beaver then turned to Jim 'I think you've just been drafted son, you're the new lead singer in this band'.

18

LIGHT BULB HEAD AND MADRAS MAN

You couldn't walk a block without hearing "Get a hair cut!" from a passing car.

In the years 1964 through 1969 Sharon schools had a very strict dress code. Here's an example of a letter we'd get at the beginning of every school year. The Beatles rated high in the code: No Beatle hair cuts, No Beatle boots or collarless jackets, no tennis shoes, no cleats on shoes, no hair touching the shirt collar, no hair touching eyebrows, no hair touching the ears, no side burns or facial hair of any kind, no blue jeans, no checked or striped pants, no cowboy boots and for girls no skirts or dress more than 2" over the knee and no culottes. The Catholic high schools were a lot less strict. We went to work immediately to circumvent these outrageous rules with some very clever ideas. Short haired wigs was one of the best ones.

In an act of defiant civil disobedience that would have made Gandhi proud, Lou Meyers shaved his head bald and walked into school with an opened umbrella. In my protest, I dressed in all different kinds of Madras: A Madras hat, shirt, tie, belt, sports jacket and trousers. It looked insane and ridiculous and I was immediately suspended for three days as was Lou. The reason they'd always put on our suspension slips was "insubordination" which I thought was hilarious. Then suddenly in 1970 for no particular reason the dress code was pretty much abolished and relegated to the dust bin of Sharon High School history.

MADRAS MAN (A Blues In 3/4 Time)

(Frank Secich)

I was walking on my hands
On the rail of the Oakland Avenue Bridge
A dream fell from my pocket and
Sailed west over the Ohio ridge
I looked up at Highway 62 below
Where I saw a dust devil up and blow
Around a pile of autumn leaves into a perfect cameo for
Madras Man and the Herringbone
Girl of his dreams but she and her
Madras Man were about to come apart at the seams

I saw Sherlock Holmes with a magnifying glass
He said "I have recovered your dream"
In an overgrown field called Circustown
With burgundy buildings made of corrugated steel
A trap door opened, someone hit me from behind
The next I know I'm on my way to Shanghai
The crew were keel-hauling.... an albatross
They already had a fire and some barbecue sauce
When they saw
Madras Man but the image did not compute

What looked so much like
Madras Man all decked out in a hounds tooth diving suit

I took the lure of the carnival
The "Scrambler" and the "Tilt-A-Whirl"
On the midway I heard a barker call
It was Robert Preston, he was 30 feet tall
I paid the fee but was a little uncertain
Then was struck in awe when they opened the curtain
Revealing Madras Man wearing Chinese finger cuffs
A sad, weeping Madras Man crying Paisley tears into a cup

The gypsy girl said "I'm here to warn ya
To stay away from that girl from California
I said "I don't know what you're talkin' about . . .
I've never been there"
She said "you will to both so you'd better beware"
Through the back of my head
I saw her shivering and crying
As I was overcome by Mohair and wine
Just when I thought that all was good and fine
I saw Madras Man out there lying in the west coast sun
Most definitely Madras Man doing something that he
never should have done

Just when things could not get more out of hand
I put a cherry bomb in your garbage can
The sound was heard for a mile or two
Damaged the garbage in the process too
A reporter was called there was nothing left to chance
In his mackintosh coat and matching continental pants
He got real excited, did a holy roller dance
Took out a highlighter that he shoplifted in France
With no warning in advance went into a trance
Wound up like Bobby Shantz then he brought the heat
And threw it at Madras Man who jumped out of his
Nailed on shoes
A mound charging Madras Man, halfway home
With a broken banjo playing a three four time blues

19

THE LOCAL SCENE OF 1965-1968 – THE BANDS

One of the biggest influences on us at the time was the local scene. There were tons of great groups you could usually see for anywhere between 75 cents and a $1.25 Here are a few that played locally in Sharon, Warren, Ohio and Youngstown all the time. The Human Beinz (who had the worldwide hit *Nobody But Me* in 1967-69, Phil Keaggy's Squires, Volume IV, New Hudson Exit and then Glass Harp 1966-69, The famed 'Poppy' with Roger Lewis, Mark Dehr, Danny Pecchio and Dick Strojny 1967-68, The Holes In The Road from Warren Ohio who were the best Ohio band of all-time in my opinion 1966-69 with Shel Downs, Joe Saker, Gary Sloas, Dave Pack, Gary McCoy and Doug Thomas. Later in 2003 Doug Thomas and Gary McCoy along with Gary's brother Tommy McCoy would team up with Levon Helm and Garth Hudson and do the fabulous Howlin' Hill Project. The James Gang with Joe Walsh, The Cyrus Erie with Eric Carmen, Wally Bryson and the McBride Brothers 1967-1969, The Choir (*It's Cold Outside*), The Executioners, The Next Of Kin (with Jerry Centifanti), The Prophets, Peck's Bad Boys (Terry Demaria, David Magnotto), The King's V (Mike Pinti), The Pied Pipers, Menagerie (Terry Demaria, Bobby Paoletta), Salt (John Morell), The Schillings, 215 City Blues, Freeman Sound (John Harrow, Kurt Sunderman), The Fabulous Fantastics, The Bell Boys, The Chylds (with Joe Vitale), The Insights, Clockwork Blues, The Shades of Rhythm (with future Blue Asher's Bill 'Cupid' Bartolin and Bill 'Goog' Yendrek), The Blues Option, The Collection (with Steven Acker), Mother Goose Band, Jan Mac and the Fruits Of Love (John Hanti, Jan McIntire), Jim Gustafson (Biggie Rat, Poobah) and Sound Barrier (Paul Hess) and many more I could list.

20

THE LOCAL SCENE OF 1966-1968 – THE VENUES

There were a wide variety of teens clubs and over drinking age clubs (18 was the legal drinking age in Ohio for beer) to play as well. For the teens in Ohio it would be the Carousel Teen Clubs in McKinley Heights, Hubbard, Youngstown on Midlothian and more. Packard Music Hall in Warren ran regular dances as did Champion Rollarena, Lake Villas, Christ Episcopal Church, Howland Community Church right down the road. In Sharon and Brookfield we had Yankee Lake Ballroom in Brookfield and St. Joe's, Our Lady Of Fatima, The Bug Out, The American Legion, The Girl's Buhl Club and The Buhl Farm Casino in Buhl Park and many many others including all the area high schools who always had dances and record hops with "live" bands.

From the local scene out of the 60's into the 70's quite a few local bands were signed to major labels and had national exposure: Human Beinz on Capitol Records, Raspberries signed to Capitol Records, Blue Ash signed to Mercury Records and then to Playboy Records, Glass Harp signed to Decca Records, Left End to Polydor Records, Law with Steve Acker signed to MCA Records, Poobah with Jim Gustaffson, Dead Boys on Sire Records, Rubber City Rebels on Capitol Records, Menagerie on Mercury Records, Chrissie Hynde, Maureen McGovern (The Morning After from the Poseidon Adventure), Myron Grombacher (drummer with Pat Benetar), Bob DiPiero (major country hit songwriter), Joe Walsh (James Gang and the Eagles), Greg Reeves (CSN&Y) and later Trent Reznor of Nine Inch Nails (one of the kids who used to hang out in National Record Mart when I managed it) were just some of the famous musicians you could see at the local clubs and teen halls back then.

21

1967 – THE TIME OF TROUBLE STARTS

The year of 1966 came to a smashing close for me. I knew I had a choice to make between a musical career or a criminal career. It was a close run thing. 1967 appeared and hit me hard. My girlfriend, Mary Jean broke up with me over the telephone. My school work was an abject failure and I was in trouble with the law over a myriad of rumors and accusations. Half the jocks and hoods in the valley wanted to kill me. My most serious problem consisted of leveled charges of breaking into an abandoned house in the woods near us and using it for a party place. Spiraling down the vortex, I was headed for Juvenile Court in February and afterward most likely straight to the Reform School at the George Junior Republic in Grove City, PA. My future was not wide open.

At Juvenile Court we stood before the judge to answer to the charges as the owner of the old house testified to and exaggerated the damages. Judge McKay then started talking to each one of us. Some of the boys had lawyers there as well. Beaver and I didn't and did not dress in suits but wore some of our best mod clothes. The trial was all sort of a surreal Fellini movie kind of Toby Damitt affair to me. Suddenly the judge called my name 'Frank Secich.... Are you sorry you did it or are you sorry you got caught?' 'To tell you the truth, Judge. 'I'm sorry I got caught'. 'Well Sir!' You're one of the few honest men who have ever stood before me in this court. Some of you boys here are actually looking forward to reform school as though it would be some kind of adventure or badge of honor. It's not! So, I'm not sending you there. You'll be on probation for one year and will work hard fixing up at the house on weekends and furnish the materials to do it'.

We were still allowed to play in the band and started picking up better gigs Sharon Country Club, Patty Costello's Party, Cathy Hainley's Party, Girl's Buhl Club, First United Methodist Church Battle Of The Bands, St. Anne's Summer Fete and a few others. Sequestered to home at night the band slowly started falling apart. I occasionally still did the odd job with them. Beaver and I had a lot of time to practice on guitar and singing harmonies. Jim, Beaver and I could do the Four Seasons (who we all hated) acapella perfectly walking about town. *Rag Doll* or *Dawn* note for note for a piss-take. On probation we were allowed to go the dances. Beaver and I would still stand in front of the already legendary local guitar gods like Roger Lewis from the Poppy and Phil Keaggy from the New Hudson Exit and watch what they were playing and try and pick up riffs. We went to see a lot of bands like the Holes In The Road and Human Beinz but we were still nowhere even in the same league as those guys.

There were two records that February that really saved my life. They were the American Version of the Rolling Stones *'Between The Buttons'* LP and *'Strawberry Fields Forever/Penny Lane'* single by the Beatles. Just when everything in my life had turned to shit, the two greatest records in the world in my opinion were released. When in 2010 *The Staircase Stomp!* by the Deadbeat Poets became a hit on Sirius XM at Little Steven's Underground Garage, I had the great honor of corresponding with the legendary Andrew Loog Oldham manager and producer of the Rolling Stones. I got to tell him just how much *Between The Buttons* meant to me and how much it inspired me and literally changed and saved my life. I also told him how much I loved the Scottish group The Poets who Andrew also managed, discovered and produced in addition to Marianne Faithfull and the Rolling Stones. I told Andrew, I always loved their name and they were a great inspiration along with "The Big Lebowski" in me naming the Deadbeat Poets. Three days later I get a lovely email from George Gallacher (the lead singer of the Poets) as Andrew had told him my story. George and I became fast friends and pen pals for a couple of years and he sent me tons of rare Poets' songs and film and I would send him all the Deadbeat Poets and Blue Ash releases. Sadly, George died of cardiac failure on August 25, 2012 while driving home from Firhill Park after watching his beloved Partick Thistle FC beat Dumbarton 3-0. We had planned to get together the next time the Deadbeat Poets were in Scotland. I miss him and regret that I never got to meet him in person.

During my probation in 1967, I had a lot of time to practice and to attempt to write songs. I actually wrote a few good ones at that time I *Thought I Knew You, Silver Horses* and *Everywhere I Go* and more. I would still awkwardly run into Mary Jean in school and out throughout the first part of 1967 then her family moved to Pittsburgh that summer and I only saw her a couple of times after that. Beaver's father was also transferred to Pittsburgh as well by Westinghouse and they left the valley the following year 1968. That chapter of my life had ended and I narrowly escaped but my luck was soon about to change for the better.

22

MR. MARKS AND THE EPIPHONE CASINO

In the Spring of 1967, I got an after school hours and summer job at Metz Bakery next to the aforementioned beer distributor. It was hard work unloading 100lbs sacks of flour and sugar and 50lbs cubes of butter, margarine and lard and barrels of creams and jelly from semi-trucks and stacking them in an attached warehouse and then taking them into the bakery as needed. It was backbreaking work. Right after I started working I noticed the most beautiful guitar I had ever seen in the window of Marks Music in Farrell, PA. It was a cherry red Epiphone Casino just like the sunburst Casinos the Beatles were using at the time. It was $330.00. I knew my parents could never afford it.

I went and talked to Mr. Marks and told him I'd like to buy that guitar and that I have a job for the summer and I clear about $40.00 a week. I asked him if I would sign my paycheck over to him every week could I have the guitar after I made all the payments. He agreed to it, which I couldn't believe. So every week I would take my check and put it down on the guitar. After the third payment as I was leaving the store, Mr. Marks called over to me 'Hey Secich, You forgot something' he walked over to me and handed me the guitar and case. He said 'You're a good kid and I know you'll pay it off. Have fun with it'.

I was overjoyed to say the least and paid it off in time. I was 15 years old, about to turn 16 and now had my first proper electric guitar. I was motivated as hell. I also made the decision to be a professional musician rather than a professional criminal. It was a close call but the right move.

That summer Marty Magner had asked me to join his band the San Francisco Morgue which would morph into the Great Hibiscus. That line-up was Marty, Steve Routman (the guy who taught me how to play bar chords), Chuck Borawski, Ken Antos and Bruce Hickey and later John Hanti. In the matter of a few months I would meet two guys who would loom large in my life and career. I would become close friends with both Stiv Bators and Geoff Jones, two men who would take me on a great adventure.

23

THE BATTLE OF THE BANDS

In early December 1967 our band The Great Hibiscus (Ken Antos, myself, Marty Magner, Bruce Hickey and Chuck Borawski) and formerly The San Francisco Morgue made our debut at the Battle Of The Bands at Farrell PA High School Gym/Auditorium in front of about 1500 teenagers from all over the Shenango Valley. Others on the bill were the Wexford Manor (with future Blue Ash guys Bill 'Cupid' Bartolin and Bill 'Goog' Yendrek) who were great. The Sounds Of Soul (with Dean Leonetti) who were very professional and won the battle, Dave Killa Orchestra who came in second and some band from Grove City that did the Turtles' *She's My Girl* note for note which is almost impossible to sing that song as good as Howard Kaylan did.

The Great Hibiscus was the opening band. Dick Thompson from WHOT announced us. 'Here they are, the Kings of Flower Power...The Great Hibiscus'. As the curtains opened I could see a riser in the middle of the gym and crowd with the sitting judges: old guys from the musician's union and music teachers and band directors from various high schools in the valley. We had borrowed tons of amps and had a wall of speakers 8 feet tall behind us. As we hit first chord of *Interstellar Overdrive*, all the judges at once held their hands to their ears and had looks of absolute horror on their faces. I thought I'd die laughing it was so loud. We were jumping around like mad men and played one of the most anarchic versions of that song ever for ten minutes then went in to Purple Haze. It was one of my favorite rock and roll experiences. We were only 16 years old. I wish I had a recording of it

24

ST. JOE'S CAROUSEL TEEN CLUBS

As I had previously mentioned during probation we were allowed to go the dances. We went to see a lot of bands like the Holes In The Road and Human Beinz who we idolized. Now in 1967 and 1968 many of us had driver's licenses and cars. We were now mobile and could go easily to Youngstown and Warren to see bands as well as Cleveland. A bunch of would go to the local teen clubs and dances and hang out: Geri Jones (Geoff's sister), Stiv Bators, Marty Magner, Carol Moll, Joann Rose (who was my new girlfriend), Mike Miller and Karen (Carothers) Wagner.

We would travel as far as the Mentor and Chesterland Hullabaloo clubs. John Hanti our keyboardist was a great hustler and managed to get the Great Hibiscus some prestigious gigs. St. Joe's was one of the best places to play. It had perfect acoustics and was always filled with kids. They'd always have two bands. This night the Great Hibiscus opened for the New Hudson Exit which was Phil Keaggy's band who were great and the most popular band at St. Joe's. We knew we couldn't match them talent wise but we could definitely put on a wild anarchic show. I smashed my 12-string to pieces that night, being a novice in the art of guitar annihilation, I hadn't previously loosened the strings. As I axed the first blow to the stage with all my might a couple of the strings broke and ripped my face like razors. Now I'm really pissed and bleeding and the feedback is howling like demons from hell from my amplifier. I went nuts on that guitar and the crowd was loving it. I threw all the pieces in the audience and as we finished dove head first off the stage into the crowd to a massive ovation. We were always a hard act to follow. What we didn't have in talent we more than made up for it with enthusiasm and artistic anarchy and nihilism. John also got us into Champion Rollarena and the Kinsman American Legion as well as playing all night 1967-68 New Year's Eve at Kennedy Christian High School.

25

MR. BELVEDERE – GEOFF JONES

Geoff Jones would become one of my best friends ever. We auditioned for and I first met Geoff Jones that very same December of 1967 when John Hanti got us an audition at the Carousel Teen Club in Youngstown. It was also the first time I'd encounter Stiv Bators who was a couple of years older than me and already in college at the then Youngstown University. Geoff Jones: 'So how did you come up with the name the Great Hibiscus?' Frank: 'You've never heard of the Great Hibiscus?, You really don't know?' Geoff amused: 'No, I never have?'

I explained that it was a famous biplane in World War One flown by the grandfather of Don Ho known as Grandpa Ho of the Royal Hawaiian Air Force which was the very little known tropical arm of the Lafayette Escadrille. It was the last airplane shot down by Baron von Richthofen before he was shot down himself and killed near Amiens, France on the 21st of April 1918. It had a pineapple surrounded by tiny bubbles painted on one side of it's fuselage and an Hawaiian Hibiscus on the other. I named the band in honor of it. Geoff thought I was a nut and gave us a date at the Carousel Teen Club in Youngstown.

Geoff was like the big brother I never had. My Mom and Dad adored him. He gave me a chance to be a professional musician at the ripe age of 18 and probably kept me out of jail and alive. You never would have heard about Blue Ash or Glass Harp or me or Stiv Bators without him. Geoff was Blue Ash's manager from start to finish, ran a booking agency, record company and management company, was a first class photographer, a concert promoter, started Glass Harp, Blue Ash, managed Club Wow and the Infidels and was road manager for the Dead Boys. He helped countless musicians from our area. I used to tease him and call him "Mr. Belvedere" after the Clifton Webb character in the movies. He was just like him. Smarter than anyone, could take a car apart and put it together by scratch, do the Times crossword puzzle in 10 minutes like James Bond, could fix anything mechanical or electrical, build anything, solve any problem, a walking encyclopedia and could kick anyone's ass just like the Clifton Webb character. I'm actually writing a song called *Mr. Belvedere* about him. His favorite song of mine was a Beatlesque ballad called *Dark Grey Afternoon* and he always wanted Blue Ash to record it on every record. I'll have to do that some day. Geoff will return again and again throughout this story.

26

STIV BATORS – 1967

December of 1967 was a big month for me for meeting friends that would last a lifetime. The very week I met Geoff Jones, I met Stiv Bators. I met Stiv at a house on Lincoln Ave. across from the university where some students were living. We became fast friends. Stiv would become sort of my replacement in the Mother Goose band in 1970. They became a very different and theatrical band. I have a very rare film of the Mother Goose Band of that era with Stiv, Marty Magner, Terry Murcko and Mick Baldauf. They were playing at the Zodiac Club in Vienna, Ohio and had a small marching band join them made up of Steve Routman, Chuck Borawski, Dennis Hoagland and Mike Miller wearing Sharon High band uniforms and playing horns.

They then brought in a sacrificial virgin (Karen Carothers Wagner) and the film is hilarious. It's an arty and surreal film and well done. I gave a copy to Karen before she passed away and also to Stiv's parents. Later Stiv and different versions of Mother Goose would open up dozens of times for Blue Ash until Stiv went to Cleveland and formed Frankenstein and then the Dead Boys. Stiv will reappear consistently in these pages and no doubt entertain you throughout this entire book.

27

THE GREEN MAN, RAY ROBINSON

The Green Man was a real person named Ray Robinson aka Charlie No Face. I knew him when I was a teenager and in my early twenties. He was born in 1910 and died in 1985. As a boy of nine years old he was horribly disfigured in an electrical accident. He would only come out at night and would roam the spooky, dark roads of western Pennsylvania where I lived. My friends and I knew where he would hang out and we would bring him beer and cigarettes and talk to him.

I even took Stiv Bators there a few times when we were teenagers. Geoff Jones and I went there often as well in the early seventies. I have some photos of him. Ray "The Green Man" was legendary in our area. Many stories and legends are about him.

Many people think he was a myth or urban legend but he was very real.

While visiting him we would always stop at a place on Route 18 in Mahoningtown called The Haunted House. It was run by a character named Doc who looked like the devil and carried a pitchfork, no it was actually a trident I think and his assistant The Count who had two different colored eyes and a clubfoot. They had a human skeleton sitting at the inside entrance who they named George. It was considered suicidal bad luck to touch George. Doc had a yellowed newspaper article hung behind George that told of 3 teenagers from Grove City who had been to visit the Haunted House and two were killed in an auto accident on their way home. Doc always claimed those kids had touched and mocked George. For 50 cents you could tour the 3 story Haunted House that was sort of a Funhouse. The song *The Green Man* is a collection of my memories of Ray and the Haunted House. I first met Ray Robinson when I was 16 years old in 1967.

The Green Man by the Deadbeat Poets 2007 from 'Notes from The Underground' on Pop Detective Records

THE GREEN MAN 2007

(Frank Secich)

Let's go down to see the green man
Let's go down to see the green man

Hey Ray, what do you say
Let's go down to Beaver Falls today
We'll go down 18 and on the way
Stop and see Doc and the Count who's lame
With one eye gray and one eye blue
Just don't touch George whatever you do

Let's go down to see the green man

Is that you Ray? on the side of the hill
We've got some Stroh's and time to kill
Can you tell us of the accident in graphic style
What's glowing in the dark out about a mile
In the house below the road it's pitch black blue
Just don't tell George whatever you do

Let's go down to see the green man

Fay Wray, what do you say?
I hear they're showing off King Kong today
But I'm playing a trumpet in a coffin
In an upstairs room looking at bullet holes
In the ceiling from a 22
Doc, don't forget your pitchfork when they come for you
Just don't mention George whatever you do

I hear that Ray died today
Let's drink to him one more time
Raise your glass but remember to
Not touch George whatever you do

28

A TRIP TO THE PSYCHEDELIC GAS STATION AND THE ELECTRIC ZOO – 1968

After the Great Hibiscus' rhythm guitarist was killed in an automobile accident, we regrouped as a 4-piece unit: Marty Magner (lead guitar), John Hanti (organ), David Magnotto (drums) and me on bass guitar. We rechristened ourselves the Underground Depression. We hooked up with The Lysergic Mushroom (Mike Pinti, Tom Tyran, Tony Rossi, Gary Sparks and Frank Zocole) to rent a practice/rehearsal facility. In February of 1968 halfway between Sharon and Charleston on Route 62 there was a closed down Mobil Gas Station for rent for $40.00 a month, so we started rehearsing there right away.

We painted the whole inside with Day-Glo colors and installed black lights for the atmosphere. All varieties of police would come by and check it out every day even though we were out in the country and didn't have many neighbors to annoy. Still the PA state police would drop in once a day or the Hickory cops and even the Mercer County Sheriff and Jefferson Township fuzz would pop in asking 'What is this place?', Me: 'It's a Psychedelic Gas Station' and they would just scratch their heads.

Would be customers would also pull up to the empty pumps. 'Fill her up with high test and where's the head?' To which we'd reply 'It's not that kind of gas station'. It was a very cool place to rehearse as it was like a night club. There was also a hydraulic lift that worked and a cigarette machine filled with smokes that had been there since 1962. We called them '62 bummers cause they tasted so bad and had little brown spots on the white cigarette paper for sitting there for 6 years in all sorts of weather.

I had just bought my first car, a 1961 Chevy Corvair convertible so I would stay nights at the gas station to watch and protect the equipment then drive to school in the morning. We took turns doing that but I did it the most. A few month's later we got a summer's gig at Geneva-On-The Lake so we gave up the gas station.

In 2007, John Hanti and I went back to visit the spot where it was. It was leveled and nothing there but a dirty plastic baby doll's head on a stick in the middle of the space where the building once stood.

One of the great gigs to get as a band in Ohio in the 1960's was a summer residency at Geneva-On-The-Lake, Ohio on the shores of Lake Erie. It was sort of like a Butlin's holiday camp in Great Britain where people would take a week's vacation and rent a cottage or a house right along the strip by the lake. Groups would get gigs for the whole summer. As the drinking age in Ohio was 18 the clubs would be packed all summer.

The Jaggerz and the Insights at the Cove, The Hi-Guys at Sunken Bar, The Poppy at the Psychedelic Lounge and Wayne Cochran at the Castaways, The Pack (with Mark Farner) at the Beachcomber. The Underground Depression (John Hanti, Frank Secich, Marty Magner and David Magnotto) got a gig for Memorial Day weekend 1968 in Geneva-On-The-Lake at the Electric Zoo which was a brand new teenage night club on the strip right across from Eddie's.

Mel Long and his wife, Rita ran the club. A gentleman named Spencer Wold had a head shop in the entrance of the Electric Zoo and also sold some great clothes which John Hanti and I bought from him and we looked like "The Move". We went over great that weekend and Mel hired us for the entire summer. He hated our name the Underground Depression so he changed it to the Mother Goose Band. We didn't care at all. We were 16 and 17 year old guys let loose on crowds of teenage girls who would turnover and change every week. We had our own cottage which Mel got for us and we made a ton of money. We played 7 nights a week and matinees on Saturday and Sunday. We got really good and tight as a band. My sister, Cindy and her boyfriend and future husband Don Wilpula came up to see us a lot in his Mustang. They met in Cleveland but he was from Ashtabula which is next door to Geneva. We were a cover band half-psychedelic and half-soul. We even had a record company American Music Makers out of Pittsburgh wanting to record us. We even had a manager, Mike Miller and a roadie, Bob Lyshoir our friend from high school.

I had saved enough money from playing Geneva that summer to buy a better car. I got a 1963 Plymouth Valiant and later of course I wrote a song about it. One time as Jim Kendzor and I were pushing it down E. State St. in Sharon in an attempt to clutch start it, two of our friends and Sharon High Superstars, Terry Green and Gene Turnbaugh pulled along side in their new Buick Elektra and rolled down the window shouted "Hey Secich! Get a Buick", I wrote this song about that Plymouth which sounds kind of like the Beach Boys would have sounded if they lived in Ohio, had no surf boards, no California Girls, no striped shirts, no beach, no woodies and drove shitty cars. The Geneva version of the Mother Goose Band came to a screeching halt when John Hanti and Marty Magner got into a fist fight right in front of the Electric Zoo on Labor Day Weekend of that summer of 1968.

THE PSYCHEDELIC GAS STATION

(Frank Secich)

On the outskirts of our town
There was a run down Mobil Station
That we rented for a place to play
We called it the Psychedelic Gas Station

At the psychedelic gas station
There was the real & the mirage
The sounds of Mushrooms & Mother Goose men
Fluttered in that magical garage

The grey cops walked through the door
Without as much as a knock
The brass buttons on their uniforms
Glowing in the dark
By the blue flame on the pilot light
From the center of the earth
Still everyday they hassled us
For what it was worth

At the Psychedelic Gas Station
Time climbs then it falls around
The day-glo artworks on the wall
That were there earlier now they're not

You can ride the hydraulic lift, baby go up & down (and in between)
Smoke the brown spotted cigarettes, that we found.....(in a machine)

Through the strobe light's slow motion
The elevator burned
Floating in the submarine
As the building turned

We got a gig at the Electric Zoo
We had to let station go
We piled in the yellow van
Never to return anymore

Now The Psychedelic Gas Station is
Just a memory on leveled ground
Nothing left not even a brick
All that's there is a doll's head on a stick

SHE'S MY CAR

(Frank Secich)

I got a '63 Plymouth with faded red paint
Cost three hundred dollars at the used car place
Burns oil by the barrel four balds no spare
Static radio but I don't care

She's my car oo chugga oo chugga rattle rattle
Oo chugga oo chugga backfire
Oo chugga oo chugga rattle rattle
Oo chugga oo chugga backfire

The brakes grind & squeal there's one head light
I ain't got insurance but I feel alright
Drivin' down the road there ain't nothing worse
Than backing up baby with no reverse in my car

Oo chugga oo chugga rattle rattle
Oo chugga oo chugga backfire
Oo chugga oo chugga rattle rattle
Oo chugga oo chugga backfire

The bumpers are rusty, she's running hot!
Crack in the windshield the transmission's shot
Side mirror is broken hanging on by tape
Antenna missing but she's not in bad shape

Driving down the road when before I knew
I noticed all the steam as the radiator blew
The little light said red I was feeling blue
Looked under the hood the engine's gone too
Towed it on down to the junk yard site
Crane lifted it up & dropped it right
Into the crusher for the final kill
So, if you ever see a faded little block of steel
She's my car

Oo chugga oo chugga rattle rattle
Oo chugga oo chugga backfire
Oo chugga oo chugga rattle rattle
Oo chugga oo chugga backfire

29

ANYONE HAVE A MARLBORO?

Every once in a while the Mother Goose Band would get a day or two off from playing the Electric Zoo that summer and another band would fill in like Rich Engler's Grains Of Sand. On one of those occasions we went to see the Doors that summer as well. Jim Kendzor, Sean O'Toole, Patti Luoma and myself. We were about 5 rows back from the stage at Cleveland Public Hall. It was an interesting concert. When Jim Morrison first came out, he just stood at the edge of the stage and flipped off the entire crowd for about a minute moving about and sending the finger everywhere. After a couple of numbers he said 'Anyone have a Marlboro?' Hundreds of cigarette packs of all brands hit the stage as well as pills bouncing everywhere and joints. Morrison picked up a Marlboro pack, lit a cigarette and said 'Thanks man. I do that once a year for my smokes'. A little later Morrison dove into the crowd and punched one girl near me right in the face, then the strangest thing happened. Girls were crying and yelling at him to hit them.

To this day it's still one of the sickest things I'd ever seen. In a way it was a fun and strange concert to attend and I was glad I was there. We had taken the bus to Cleveland but had no way home. We started to hitch hike on Euclid Avenue after the concert and the first car that came by picked us up. They were from Warren and had been to the concert and took us right to our homes in Sharon. What luck we had. We started going to Warren a lot to see bands like the Holes in The Road. Late that summer of 1968, I met a girl named Joann Rose at a Holes In The Road show at the Champion Rollarena and we would pretty much be together from then until early 1970.

The Plymouth served us well that year as we were now mobile especially since gasoline was 29.9 cents a gallon and half the time there were gas wars and it would be 24.9 cents a gallon and we could go farther to see bands and we did. We went to Cleveland a lot that Autumn of 1968 to see The Nazz, The Jeff Beck Group, Fever Tree, James Gang and Cyrus Erie numerous times at the Mentor Hullabaloo and Chesterland Hullabaloo, the Cleveland Teen Fairs and other venues.

30

MY MOM AND DAD – A PAIR THAT WOULD BEAT A FULL HOUSE ANYTIME

As I promised in the first paragraph of this tome more on my Mom and Dad. This was Stiv Bators' favorite story about my Dad.

When I was about 10 years old we were eating dinner and I told my Dad 'Today in school, Father told us that if we ever enter a Protestant Church or marry a Protestant it would be a sin and we could be condemned to hell forever'. My dad stopped eating, shook his head and said 'When you're in class tomorrow Frankie, raise your hand and ask him why he doesn't have a real job like everybody else?' My mother said to him 'You can't tell him to say that to a priest, what's wrong with you?' I thought it was hilarious.

My Dad was a diehard working-class Democrat but one day in the early 80's there was a knock on his door which my Dad opened 'Hi, I'm Tom Ridge and I'm running for congress'. My Dad shook his hand and said 'Well. I'll give you this.. You've got a lot of balls knocking on doors in this neighborhood'. Ridge: 'Yeah, I'm finding that out'. My Dad 'Well, I'll listen to what have you've got to say' and they talked for about 10 minutes and as he left my Dad told him he'd think about voting for him. My Dad later told me 'You know I've never voted for a Republican before but I'm going to vote for that guy. I like him.' My dad did vote for him all the way through Congress to his becoming Governor of Pennsylvania. After 911, Tom Ridge became the first Secretary of Homeland Security.

Sharon, PA where I lived and still live near is halfway between Cleveland and Pittsburgh. Loyalties are to professional sports teams the Cleveland Indians and Browns or the Pittsburgh Steelers and Pirates. The rivalry is fierce and fandom is equally distributed in our town. In some cases there are known instances of fathers and sons and brother and brother pitted against each other. Everyone seems to like the Cavs and the Penguins as there is no NBA or NHL counterpart in each city. My dad and myself were Cleveland fans. In the mid-90's when the Indians were doing very good, my Dad had Parkinson's Disease and was dying as well. Once when I was visiting him at that time I tried to cheer him up. 'What do you think, Pop? How about that Tribe? You getting pennant fever? They could really go all the way'. He opened his eyes and with a very weak voice while shaking his head negatively and said, 'Don't... Don't believe in them... They'll only break your heart... They'll never win the World Series again... I gave up on those bastards in 1959'. Even when he was deathly ill, he had a great sense of humor and irony.

My Mom was a pistol and also had a great sense on humor. One day in the mid-80's it was my Dad's birthday and we all gathered at their house. As my Dad was opening his present from my Mom, she whispered to me 'Watch your father open his birthday card'. He opened the card glanced at it for a second then opened his gift. I told her 'I don't get it?' 'He never reads my cards, just opens the gifts'. Then she said 'I noticed that years ago and I have been giving him the same birthday card for 35 years now and he's never noticed'. I miss both of them so badly and especially miss all the laughs and good times.

31

1969'S OK

After the Geneva debacle, Mother Goose regrouped with Manfred Kodilla on bass, me back to rhythm guitar, Marty Magner on lead and Terry Murcko on drums. This new Mother Goose configuration first appeared at an all-night New Year's Eve party at St. John's Episcopal Church in Sharon the night of 1968-69. This version of Mother Goose didn't last long. We played maybe a dozen gigs in January and February 1969 at the Dream Merchant in Youngstown then went 3 piece with Manfred leaving and me back on bass. At this point it wasn't fun anymore and I was writing a lot of songs and really wanted to start another band. I tried to get Jim Kendzor in the band and he auditioned for the band but Marty didn't want him. I never understood that and I really started to lose interest in the Mother Goose Band. During this time I would also take pick up gigs at coffee houses and bars with my friend Steve Acker who would later be in LAW when he would come on weekends from Mercersberg Academy. I was ready for something new.

I played my last gig with Mother Goose on Memorial Day 1969 in Cleveland at Europhia on Euclid Ave. As I was on-stage I had a lung collapse and actually finished the gig in immense pain. When I got back to Sharon the next morning I was hospitalized and spent 10 days in hospital. I had a lot of time to think and plan. A lot of my friends showed up at the hospital to visit so there was always kind of a party there, John and Bob Lyshoir, Joann Rose, Jim Kendzor, Sean O'Toole and my good friend Gwynne Allen who was also in the hospital was on the same floor as me. While I was in the hospital True Blue Saloon members Dave Volarich and Shane George asked me to join their band for the summer. They were a good band and had just put out a 45 cover of *Tin Soldier* by the Small Faces. I told them that I would fill in on bass for the summer but in September I was starting a new band with Jim Kendzor. They agreed.

On the night of July 31, 1969, We (Jim Kendzor, Chuck Perfillio, Chuck Borawski, Steve Theiss and me) drove all night of July 31 and August 1 through Pennsylvania on Route 322 and arrived where it ends at Atlantic City, New Jersey. The Atlantic City Pop Festival was fabulous. It was held at the Atlantic City Racetrack so there was plenty of food, rest rooms and it was fairly comfortable as compared with

Woodstock. I think there were 100,000 people there and was the biggest festival of it's kind until Woodstock eclipsed it a few weeks later. My girlfriend, Joann and her sister Jan met up with us the second day. The highlights for me (and I saw every one of the bands except Iron Butterfly) were Creedence Clearwater Revival, The Byrds, Janice Joplin (who I met and had a great conversation with), Mothers Of Invention, who only played one song *King Kong* for 45 minutes and the highlight of their set was Motorhead Sherwood who stood there silently with a tambourine and hit it just once at about 22:34 into the song. I thought that was genius. Paul Butterfield Blues Band just killed as did Procol Harum. Tim Buckley, Little Richard and Booker T. and the MG's were amazing as well as an unknown band named AUM who's guitarist dove off the stage which was about ten feet high and smashed his Gibson SG to pieces on the ground. It was very impressive.

Not at all impressive and the only act I didn't care for during the whole festival and I have not liked to this day was Joni Mitchell. She came out and did one song then starting getting on and berating the audience because that they weren't "listening to her". She said 'I sang the same verse twice and no one noticed'. I had never seen an artist be so condescending, pretentious and snarky to an audience and the audience feedback was swift and fierce. "Get off the fuckin' stage!", "Bring on Creedence!" "Who fuckin' cares". Then she started crying and left the stage amid thousands of boos. Everyone there was glad she did. It was a great experience all told and Jim, Chuck and I came back with tons of ideas for Blue Ash. I also met up with Beaver Warner who I hadn't seen in a while down there and we gave him a ride back home to Monroeville, PA.

32

BIRTH OF BLUE ASH

Blue Ash was actually conceived in June of 1969. It was the brainchild of me, Jim Kendzor and Chuck Borawski who was to be our bass player as he had just bought a great looking and sounding German Framus bass and I was to be rhythm guitar and Bill 'Goog' Yendrek on lead guitar. We looked all summer to find a permanent drummer and tried out many. In late July, my then girlfriend Joann Rose suggested David Evans and introduced him to me at Champion Rollarena in Champion, Ohio and he was great and worked out perfectly. Right before our first rehearsal Chuck decided he didn't want to play in the band so I took over on bass and we became a quartet. In early June, me, Jim Kendzor and our friends Denny Farringer and Dennis Fagan took a trip to Nashville to check out the music scene. On the way down we were trying to name our new band and not having any luck. After about six hours of this while driving on I71, I finally said 'Okay, that's it'. We're going to name ourselves after the next sign we see. Suddenly Jim points at a sign and says Blue Ash, which is a small town right outside of Cincinnati. We loved it. It was a good thing because we could have easily been lumbered with the moniker Wolf Ledges or worse still Gnadenhutten. We didn't care to much for Nashville but 2 good things happened. We got the name Blue Ash for the band and we wrote the first Blue Ash song *Don't Go To Nashville* which is pretty good.

So, Blue Ash (David Evans, Bill 'Goog' Yendrek, Jim Kendzor and myself) started rehearsing in late July, 1969. We took a few days off for the Atlantic City Pop Festival then started putting in 8 hours a day every day. The first song we ever learned was *I Gotta Move* by the Kinks. We wanted to be a different kind of band. We didn't like a lot of the singer songwriters and heavy and progressive bands that were omnipresent at the time. We wanted to do 3 minute songs filled with energy, harmonies, melodies and power. We did covers of our fave bands from the 60's we loved like The Beatles, Stones, Kinks, The Who. Byrds, Hollies and many others. We also did about half originals at the time as well. After about a month of rehearsals we showed up at Geoff Jones' house. Geoff was the top booking agent and band manager in Youngstown. Little did we know the day before Geoff and his top act Glass Harp featuring Phil Keaggy had just parted ways. Anyway, we asked if he'd like to be our manager then sang to him acapella *It's For You* and *Nowhere Man* nailing them perfectly and showing him we knew what we were doing. Geoff's sister, Geri and his mom, Julie were also there and pulling for us. Geoff agreed to take us on and booked our first engagement at the Freak Out in Youngstown for October 3rd, 1969.

We were really excited to have some proper management and a booking agent, we practiced like mad men all of September and were ready. There was a good buzz about us and we managed to pack the place that night. We also had been working on a great stage show segueing songs with lots of movement and flying around on stage. We changed clothes every set if we were playing 3 or 4 sets a night. We felt we had a very professional and exciting show. The first song we ever did at the Freak Out our debut night was *Wait* by the Beatles from Rubber Soul. We went over great and got steady dates at the Freak Out and Geoff sent us to Ravenna to play the next night to fill in for another band who couldn't make it. Geoff would book and manage us for over 1400 gigs and two LP's on major labels for the next ten years.

33

PARTY AT GOOG'S PAD (EVERY NIGHT)

Blue Ash set up camp and headquarters at Goog's house out in the country in Brookfield, Ohio. Goog's dad, Mike Yendrek would work the afternoon shift at the mill so we could rehearse every day from 4:00pm until midnight. Goog's mom had passed away and he had on older sister Anna who had Down Syndrome, so we could make all the noise we wanted. We called Mike Yendrek "The Great Leader" and he was a great guy who looked like Ernest Hemmingway and use to work as an artist for Walt Disney in the 1930's. So for the next year every night we weren't playing or practicing we'd be there but it was not all work as we had a constant party going during and around rehearsals. We even had a sign on State Route 7 that said "Party At Goog's" every night with a sign that pointed the way. The Cortland Girls who were great friends were out there a lot, Patty "Nugget" Hadley, Denise Dan and Stacy. There were four other pretty girls from Farrell who would also hang out at Goog's. They were called "The Greeks" though only sisters Dora and Toula Nicholas were really Greek. Darla Dudash and Maria Grkinich were the other two. Darla later married Bill 'Cupid' Bartolin from Blue Ash and Maria married Eddie Jobson the famous violinist and keyboardist with Curved Air, Roxy Music, Yes and Jethro Tull.

We met many people who would just show up out of curiosity. Geoff started getting us some great gigs at The Bug Out in Transfer, PA where the legendary Boots Bell from WHOT was DJ and compere and Champion Rollarena where WHOT's Johnny Kay was DJ and master of ceremonies. Champion was the first place Blue Ash ever did John Lennon's *Cold Turkey*. Jim and I were in my Plymouth by the university when we first heard it. We decided we would end our show with it and just go nuts with it every time never knowing where it would end up. The first time we did it at Champion the kids went nuts and stormed the stage we got rousing ovations and encores. Johnny Kay and Boots Bell would promote us like crazy on their radio shows. 'You've got to see these guys to believe it' and with their help we got very well known our first year.

One of the cool things that Geoff did was get us copies of the Beatles *Let It Be* LP about 9 months before it was ever released so we were doing *I, Me, Mine, I Dig A Pony, I've Got A Feeling* and all of them before anyone had ever heard of them. Geoff also went on WHOT with Dick Thompson one night and played it and they got a cease and desist order from Capitol Records within half an hour. Geoffrey had a friend at Apple Records who sent him the tapes. He never did say who it was but it was very cool to hear and play those Beatles songs before anyone in the world.

34

DAVID EVANS – EVAN HANLEY

All the drummers I ever played with were tough guys: Johnny Blitz, Jeff Rozniata, Kenny Antos, Dave Magnotto, Shane George, Terry Murcko, David Quinton Steinberg, Bobby Tocco, George Grexa, Rick Bremmer, John Koury and David Evans who was also known as Evan Hanley.

One time we were playing at The Freak Out when Jim forgot the words to the song we were doing. He would do this more than once in the beginning then he'd look over at me as if there was something I could do about it. I looked back at David and he's still playing but holding and waving a drumstick around in his right hand like he was going to throw it. He had extra heavy drumsticks that looked like billy clubs. All of the sudden he takes aim and throws it right at Jim and hits him in the back of the head. Stunned, Jim turns around and dives over the drums and they start beating the shit out of each other, drums, sticks, fists and cymbals flying everywhere. The funny thing was Cupid and I never stopped playing and while still playing watched in disbelief. After about 30 seconds of fisticuffs they realized they were fighting on stage in front of 400 people, so the roadies and Jim and David start setting the fallen drums back up and as Cupid and I were still playing they joined right in the song and we finished like nothing happened. The audience gave us a huge ovation as if it were some kind of stage act.

My grandfather John Abranovich's band in Johnstown, PA the 1920's. John is the bass player.

My dad, Frank upper left and his brothers in World War II.

My mom, Dolly 1966

Mrs. Verraux's Second Grade Class at Wengler School
Sharon, PA 1958-59

1st Row Seat 1: Mark 'Beaver' Warner, **Seat 4:** Frank Secich
2nd Row Last Seat: Gayle Holland
3rd Row Seat 4: Mary Jo Chizmar
5th Row Seat 3: Chuck Borawski

In High School with slicked back hair to avoid suspension.

Left Eye 3, The City Jail 1967 St. Ann's Picnic Farrell, PA. Billy Rudge, Frank Secich, Jim Kendzor, Jeff Rozniata, Scott Deans and Mark 'Beaver' Warner.
Photo: Marion Rozniata

Blue Ash Day One July 1969 in Brookfield, Ohio. Bill 'Goog' Yendrek, David Evans, Jim Kendzor and FrankSecich.   Photo: Darla Bartolin

Blue Ash. Jim Kendzor and Frank Secich at the Bug Out, in Transfer, PA October, 1969.   Photo: Maryann Secich Hartmann

Blue Ash at the Girl's Buhl Club, Sharon PA October, 1969 Bill 'Goog' Yendrek, Jim Kendzor, David Evans and Frank Secich.
Photo: Denise Dan Litton

Blue Ash Publicity Photo 1971. Frank Secich, Jim Kendzor, Bill 'Cupid' Bartolin and David Evans. Photo: Geoff Jones

Blue Ash and Tiny Tim 1971 in Youngstown, Ohio. Jim Kendzor, Frank Secich, Tiny Tim and David Evans

Blue Ash recording at Peppermint 1972. David Evans, Jim Kendzor, Gary Rhamy of Peppermint, Frank Secich and Bill 'Cupid' Bartloin.

Paul Nelson and Geoff Jones in Idora Park, Youngstown 1973.
Photo: Frank Secich

Blue Ash in Youngstown, 1973. Jim Kendzor (standing), David Evans, Frank Secich and Bill 'Cupid' Bartolin. Photo: David Gahr

Frank Secich, Yoko Ono and Jim Kendzor at Kenny's Castaways, New York City October 1973. Photo: Geoff Jones

Blue Ash 1974. Frank Secich, Jim Kendzor, Bill 'Cupid' Bartolin and Jeff Rozniata.
Photo: Geoff Jones

Blue Ash 1974. Photo: Geoff Jones

Blonde Stiv and Tim Comer in Youngstown, Ohio 1977 wearing a Blue Ash Tee Shirt.
Photo: Theresa Kereakes

Stiv Bators and Frank Secich at JB's in Kent, Ohio 1979. Photo: Kal Mullens

Stiv Bators 'Its Cold Outside' photo shoot April 1979 Stiv Bators, Rick Bremmer, Frank Secich and Eddy Best. Photos: Donna Santisi

Stiv Bators and Frank Secich LA 1979. Photos: Donna Santisi

Stiv Bators and Frank Secich LA 1979. Photos: Donna Santisi

Greg Shaw, Frank Secich, Stiv Bators and David Zammit recording *It's Cold Outside* and *The Last Year* April 1979 W. Hollywood Bijou Studio. Photo: Theresa Kereakes

Mick Rock's picture sleeve for "Not That Way Anymore" Frank Secich and Stiv Bators.

Bomp publicity photo 1980. Frank Secich, Jimmy Zero, Stiv Bators, Johnny Blitz and George Cabaniss

Author Cynthia Heimel, Stiv Bators, Bebe Buell and Frank Secich at Bebe's Birthday Party, Mudd Club New York City - 07/14/1979

Dead Boys Backstage at the Whisky A Go-Go 01/25/80. John Belushi, Stiv Bators and Frank Secich. Photo: Donna Santisi

Frank Secich, Susan Sarandon, Stiv Bators and Jimmy Zero at the Gramercy Hotel NYC 1980. Photo: Geoff Jones

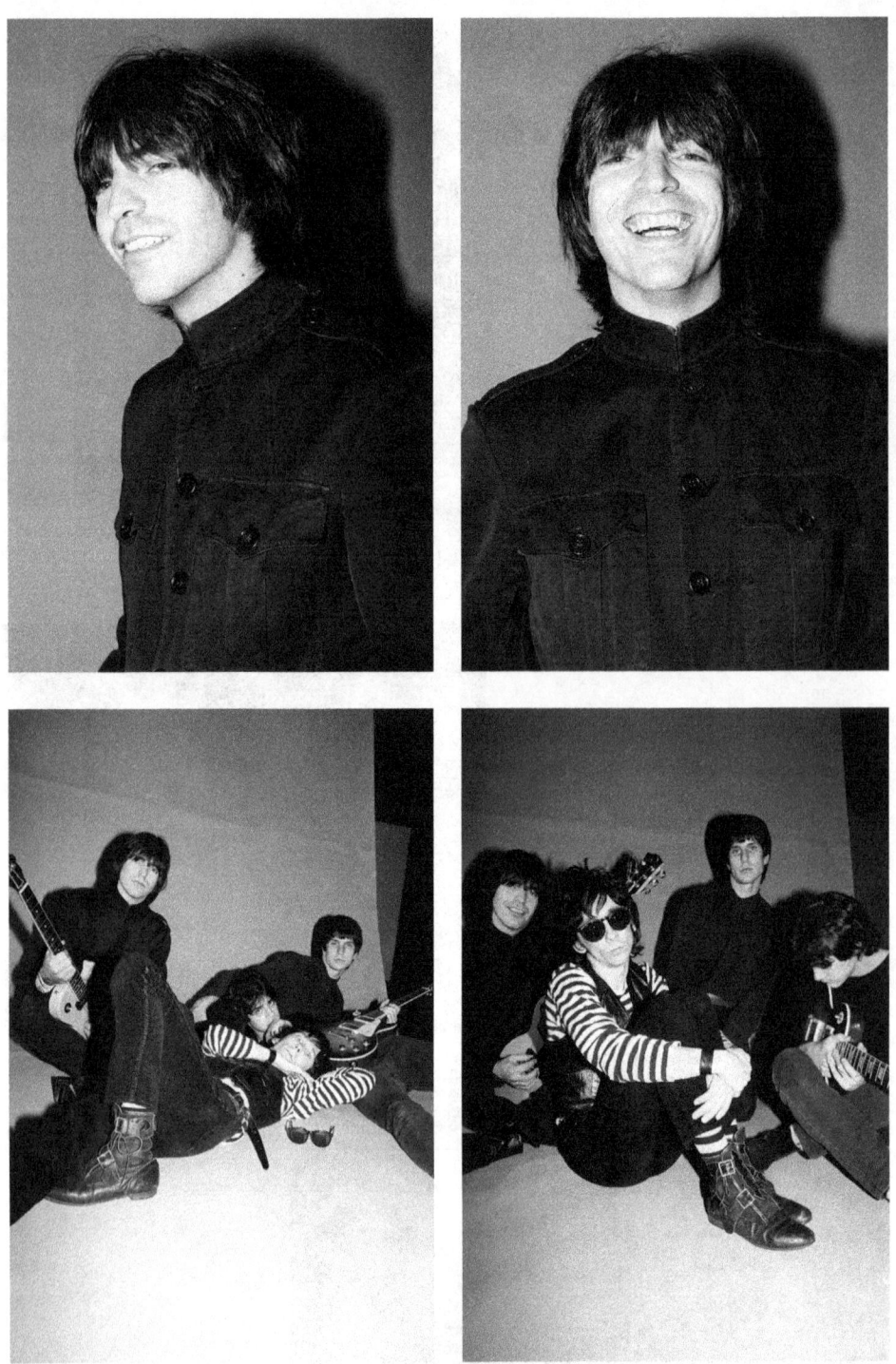

Stiv Bators 'Disconnected' album photo shoot 1980. Frank Secich, Stiv Bators, David Quinton Steinberg and George Cabaniss. Photos: Theresa Kereakes

Stiv Bators, Frank Secich, David Quinton Steinberg, George Cabaniss and Jimmy Zero outside the Uncle Floyd TV Show in Newark, NJ May 1980. Photo: Geoff Jones

Frank and Lisa Secich 1982

Club Wow 1982 at Pirate's Cove Cleveland. Billy Sullivan, Jeff West, Jimmy Zero and Frank Secich. Photo: Lisa Secich

Club Wow 1982. Billy Sullivan, Frank Secich, Jeff West and Jimmy Zero. Photo: Steve Scott

Club Wow at the Phantasy Cleveland 1983. Billy Sullivan, Jeff West, Frank Secich and Jimmy Zero. Photo: Steve Scott

National Record Mart Man Frank Secich 1984

The Infidels And Their Manager 1984. Tony Mentzer, John Koury, Pete Drivere, Frank Secich and John Hlumyk. Photo: Geoff Jones

Frank and Lisa 1985

Recording the Deadbeat Poets *Hallelujah Anyway* in 2014 at Ampreon Recorder in Youngstown. Photo: John Koury

Deadbeat Poets 2014 Terry Hartman, Pete Drivere, Frank Secich and John Koury.
Photo: Chris Rutushin

Deadbeat Poets in Stockholm, Sweden January 2012. John Koury, Pete Drivere, Terry Hartman and Frank Secich. Photo: Tommy Sjostrom

Deadbeat Poets in Prague, Czech Republic at Charles Bridge. Joe Sztabnik, Hilary Hodgson, Terry Hartman, Pete Drivere, Frank Secich and Cynthia Ross. Photo: John Koury

FrankSecich at the Kaiserkeller in Hamburg, Germany January 2012   Photo by John Koury

Mark Hershberger from Pop Detective Records

Frank and Jake Secich in Washington Square Park Greenwich village 2011.
Photo by Mark Hershberger

Mark Hershberger, Jake Secich (my son), Handsome Dick Manitoba and Frank Secich outside of Manitoba's Bar in New York City 2011.

Frank and Tucker
2015

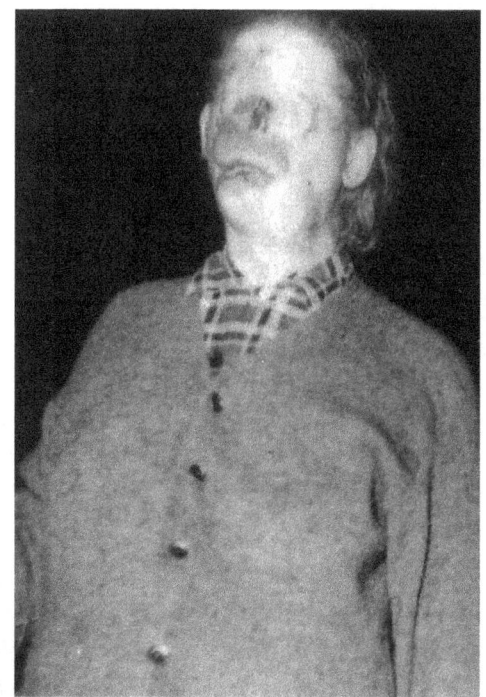
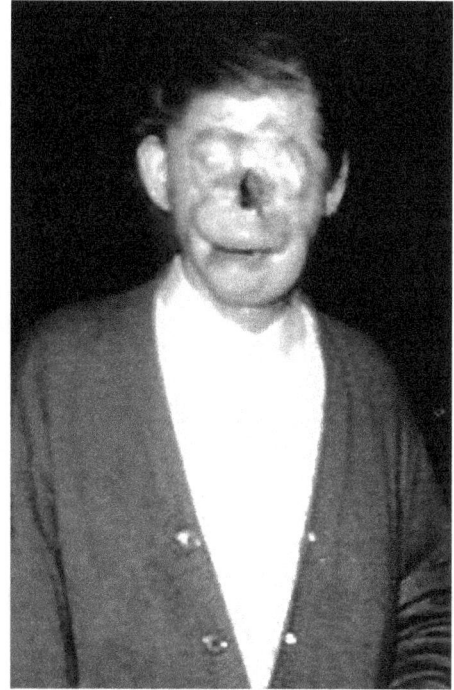

Photos of Ray Robinson, The Green Man. Left Photo: Frank Secich

35

CHUCK BERRY - CLEVELAND PUBLIC HALL MARCH 26 - 1970

On Thursday March 26, 1970 the 1950's Rock and Roll Revival came to Cleveland's Public Hall. It had an all-star line-up: Chuck Berry, Bill Haley, Bo Diddley, The Coasters, The Drifters, The Shirelles and all backed by the Bobby Comstock Band who were great. Geoff Jones knew the concert promoter well so we begged Geoff to get us great tickets. He got us 4 tickets in the first row right up front. Jim Kendzor, our roadies Newt Iliff, Joe 'Lice' Harris and myself went to the show. We all had leather jackets on for some reason. Geoff was backstage with the promoter. It was a bad day to begin with to have a concert there as it was a Thursday (working night) and the Moody Blues who were very hot then were right down the street at the Allen Theater for 2 shows. So, in a hall that holds 10,000 people there were about 1200 in attendance. Most of the Public Hall crowd were 30 something straight types and very laid back. There weren't many "Oldies" shows at that time because they were decidedly out of fashion. Anyway, our heroes were there right in front of us and we were there to have the time of our lives.

All of the acts the Shirelles, Coasters and Drifters sounded stellar and Bobby Comstock had a tight and swinging band. Bill Haley was amazing and Bo Diddley was fabulous but the audience was luke warm which I found very odd. When it came time for the headliner Chuck Berry to play it was 11:30pm. They made an announcement that the concert would end at midnight and go no longer as it had been running long. So with only a half hour to play Chuck took the stage and he was visibly pissed off.

He played the first tune and was out of time and tune. Hardly any reaction from the audience except for the leather jackets up front who cheered wildly. Chuck played a second song and the same crowd reaction except for us. He then walked to the edge of the stage right in front of me and called me over to him. At first I thought he was going screw with me in some way. He bent over and asked me 'What songs do you guys want to hear?' I said *Brown-Eyed Handsome Man* which he broke right into and it was amazing and the crowd started to get going. He bent back down to me 'What else?' How about *Roll Over Beethoven*? Now the crowd is starting to go crazy. This went on building for the next few songs. They finally turned on all the house lights which signaled the end of the show. Finally, Chuck broke into *Johnny B. Goode* and we all went crazy, The four of us stormed the stage first and almost all 1200 followed. It was completely crazy. The whole stage was filled with people rockin'. Newt Iliff and I were hanging on Chuck shoulders singing *Johnny B. Goode* into the microphone with him. It was the best ending I'd ever seen at any concert. Geoff Jones told me later after the show that Chuck Berry was backstage and said that was one of his best shows ever. He told the promoter I'd like to go out there and thank those guys in the leather jackets. The promoter looked at Geoff and said. 'Geoff, go out and thank your friends'. Geoff gathered us and brought us backstage where we met all our heroes. What a night.

36

WHENEVER YOU'RE TIRED OF BEING IN A CLOWN BAND

There was a famous musician in Youngstown who would always try and steal our drummer, David Evans away. I won't mention his name. He would always say to David 'Whenever you're tired of being in a clown band, give me a call?' I thought that was hilarious. Who us?..... A Clown Band? Maybe he was thinking of the times we'd open with *(Theme From) The Monkees* or a note-for-note spot on *Roses Are Red* by Bobby Vinton or when for no reason at all we'd break into *Pipeline* by the Chantays or do a rousing version of *Wooly Bully* or entertain the audience as The Four Jose Felicianos, all with shades on and rocking on stools to *Light My Fire* with Spanish accents and if we really didn't like the place it was *Release Me* by Englebert Humperdinck for twenty minutes or we'd bring Goog's sister Anna up to sing *Down By The River* or *You're A Better Man Than I*, not to mention featuring her vocal and dancing talents on *Cold Turkey* that would send shivers up your spine. Anna Yendrek was one of the greatest rock and rollers I have ever met. Anna was about ten years older than us and lived with the Great Leader and Goog. Anna had Down Syndrome. During the 1950's when she was growing up she listened to the radio constantly. You couldn't stump her on any song or artist from the Rock and Roll era. She was a savant with Rock & Roll trivia.

We took her to a lot of venues and parties with us. Our girlfriends or my sister, Maryann or the Greeks would always look after her while we played. We took her to see The Who at Cleveland Public Hall in summer of 1970. The first time we brought Anna with us to the Freak Out in Youngstown was in November of 1969 after we had played our first few jobs there. She wore a tie-dyed shirt that was printed on the back "I Love Geoff Jones". Right before we left to go play, I handed Anna a little pill. I said 'Anna, I really want you to have a great experience at the Freak Out, so take this pill. It's LSD (it was a baby aspirin), you will see all kinds of colors and things will change like magic right before your eyes. We'll all look after you so don't worry. Just relax and take it all in. She got the most devilish smile I'd ever seen on her and immediately popped the pill. The Freak Out had a great light show with all kinds of strobes and slides that were projected on the stage. Anna had the time of her life.

When it came time to leave she got on the floor and refused to move. She said she was going to live forever at the Freak Out and marry Geoff Jones. It took four guys to pick her up and put her in the van. When we got her home her father Mike was waiting up for her. 'So, Anna, how was your big night out?' She said 'I had the best time I ever had, I don't want to live here anymore. I want to live at the Freak Out and marry Geoff Jones... and I took LSD too.' I'm shaking my head and hands no to Great Leader.

We took Anna to a lot of places that year. Years later I took my wife, Lisa to Brookfield to meet Mike and Anna. He said 'Anna always talks about the year and a half you guys were here. It was the best time of her life'. Anna also had two imaginary boyfriends: "Joe The Weirdo" and "Jack Hudak". Her brother, Goog and I wrote a song called *The Ballad of Jack Hudak* which Blue Ash used to perform on stage 'live' and we even recorded it in Goog's cellar but it's been unfortunately long lost. About ten years ago in the modern internet age *The Ballad of Jack Hudak* would show up on a google search with my name attached to it. A while ago I got an email from a woman from New England whose father was named Jack Hudak and her Jack had spent some time in Ohio in the 60's. She was doing a google search on him and the song popped up. She wondered if the song was about him. I would have had a quite difficult time explaining that one. I just told her 'No, it couldn't have been about him'.

37

SUMMER SOUL SPECTACULAR – 1970

In the summer of 1970 Geoff Jones, Jim Pantelas (who owned the Freak Out) and Ralph Hessman and Eddie Alexander (Pittsburgh TV personality) put on a series of concerts in Ohio. First was Three Dog Night in Columbus which sold out and was a huge success. The next one was the Summer Soul Spectacular which featured Curtis Mayfield and the Impressions, The Intruders, Delfonics, Brenda and the Tabulations and the O'Jays. They asked me, Jim Kendzor, Henry Shaffer and David Evans to work for them as mostly gophers and roadies. The shows were in Dayton, Columbus, Akron and Youngstown. First off we had to put posters on telephone poles in all those towns. When the concerts started Henry became pretty much the gopher and the rest of us sort of roadied but they didn't have much equipment. They all sang through a Shure Vocal Master PA with 2 columns on each side and it sounded great as they didn't play that loud. Jim and I hung around mostly with Curtis Mayfield and Eddie Levert. Curtis was one of finest gentleman I've ever met. He was a real professional and very cool. One particular incident made Curtis one of my all-time heroes.

In Akron at the Civic Theater there was one fan who noticed me going back stage and back and forth through the theater. She was a cute black girl in her late teens or early twenties. She gave me a piece of paper and asked me if I could get Curtis to sign an autograph for her. She said she was one of his biggest fans and he was her idol and it would mean so much to her. I told Curtis about her and he said to bring her back stage. She was thrilled and he signed the autograph and talked to her for a few minutes like he'd known her all his life. She was practically in tears and shaking meeting him. She had a camera around her neck and Curtis said 'Girl, give your camera to Frank and come here'. He posed with her as I took half a dozen photos while he put his arm around her. I then gave her back her camera and took her back inside the theater. Once back in the theater she burst into tears. She hugged me and said 'That was just so cool, thank you so much. It was one of the coolest things I had ever seen a famous person do. It was the third greatest object lesson I ever learned. Eddie Levert was very cool too but in a different more comical way. Eddie was from Canton so when they played Akron he had tons of messages and the theater phone would ring off the hook. I said 'Eddie, here these are for you' (I had two stacks of notes an inch high) as I handed them to him, I said 'This first batch is from your relatives and friends in Canton wanting free tickets and this second batch is from women wanting you'. He took them and smiled at me and tossed them in the waste basket. He was a cool guy.

38

TOMMY

In the summer of 1970 our manager, Geoff got the great idea that Blue Ash should perform the Who's Rock Opera 'Tommy' in it's entirety and not even pause between songs. He said 'We could rent the Steelworker's Hall and have some other great groups as well like Glass Harp, Steve Bator Band and Johnny Stanko'. It was a daunting task for us. So David Evans, Bill 'Goog' Yendrek, Jim Kendzor and I set about on it. It took us a month to perfect even with practicing on days we had gigs. We segued all the songs together never having a break. The accumulative effect was amazing and you could just feel the excitement in the audience. We were never so on in our lives.

It was a risky undertaking because we couldn't tune up between songs if we had to. I remember Goog put on real heavy gauge strings on his guitar. Anyway, we pulled it off from the *Overture* straight through to *We're Not Gonna Take It*. When we got to the *See Me, Feel Me* part you could have heard a pin drop and then as we road out the chorus *Listening to you,* everyone was singing along. When we ended, the ovation was a roar. They wouldn't let us leave the stage. We did an encore of *My Generation* and then another encore of *Cold Turkey* and got off the stage and dropped exhausted in the dressing room while the cheers still went on.

Glass Harp went on next. Before they started Phil Keaggy (the gracious gentleman he's always been) said to the crowd, 'That was great, there's no way we can top that so we're just going to play our set'. Which they did and they were always fabulous.

39

BILL "CUPID" BARTOLIN JOINS BLUE ASH – 1970

Bill was my good friend and song writing partner and I miss him terribly. I had known him since we were boys long before we played in Blue Ash together. My mother and his Aunt Mary were best friends. Mary had a farm in Brookfield, Ohio and we'd often go visit and Bill and his brothers and his dad would be there a lot. We'd play on the farm by the creek and jump from the barn into hay and things like that. Later we'd meet up when we were 16 or so since we both played in bands, Bill the Shades Of Rhythm, Wanted Ones and Wexford Manor and me the Great Hibiscus and Mother Goose.

A year after Jim Kendzor, David Evans and I started Blue Ash our guitarist Bill Yendrek quit the band suddenly to go back to college, We were devastated. After a week of trying out guitarists to no avail, David, Jim and I were sitting around at my parents house and we were dejected and very down. My mother walked in the room and said 'Why don't you guys get Cupid in the band?' We just looked at each other. I grabbed the phone and called him. 'Cupid, this is Frank Sec.........(he interrupted me in mid-last name) 'I've been sitting by the telephone for a week waiting for this call, I accept'.

That was Cupid. October 3, 1970 was the first gig Bill "Cupid" Bartolin ever played with Blue Ash. October 3, 1969 was the first gig Blue Ash ever played and October 3, 1922 was my mom's birthday. October 3, 2009 was the day Bill Bartolin passed away. I miss him very deeply.

40

TINY TIM AND THE SHAH OF IRAN'S LIMOUSINE

In 1971, Jim Pantelas the owner of the "Freak Out" in Youngstown, Ohio remodeled the place and changed the name of the club to the Apartment. One of the first acts Jim brought in to kick off the new night club was Tiny Tim. Jim put Geoff Jones (who had his office in the back of the club) in charge. The were only two things Tiny Tim asked for on his rider. A limousine and 15 lettuce, tomato and mayonnaise sandwiches each day on white bread. I kid you not.

The sandwiches were easily come by but the limo was tough because it was prom season and every limo between and including Pittsburgh and Cleveland was rented. Anyway somehow through their connections they found out that the Shah Of Iran had shipped his limo to a Cleveland dealer to have a new engine put in, bullet proofed and otherwise completely overhauled. It was nearly done and ready to be shipped back to Iran. Funny thing is the only two places on earth where guys would even think of screwing with an emperor's limo and making a few bucks out of it are probably New Jersey and Ohio. Offering an offer the dealer couldn't refuse and paying him handsomely they got the limo for two days and Geoff picked up Tiny Tim and Miss Vicki at the Cleveland airport with the tray of sandwiches in the car.

The limo was amazing. The interior was all a burgundy plush velvet , there was a bar and even a sink with gold, I mean real gold faucets. The horn played the Shah's favorite tune the *Theme From The Bridge On The River Kwai* and played it very loudly. Anyway, the concert was packed and David Evans, Jim Kendzor and I got to hang out with and talk to Tiny Tim and it was still pretty early since the concert finished around midnight. Then Geoff took Tiny and Miss Vicki to their hotel and would have to take them to the Cleveland Hopkins Airport the next day and return the limo. Geoff drove back to the Apartment and Pantelas said 'Just take that limo straight to your house Geoff and put in the garage and please don't get so much as a scratch on it'. Geoff said 'Okay, Jimmy' and Pantelas leaves. Then Geoff looks at me, Kendzor and Evans and says 'Come on! There's no way we're not going joyriding in this limo around Youngstown'.

The limo was painted a gaudy copper/gold color and we took off down Market St. hanging out the open roof and yelling at people who were everywhere as the bars and clubs were still open. Then we went over to Oak Hill, Hillman and on Glenwood which is the predominantly black part of town blasting the *Bridge On The River Kwai* and screaming out the windows and roof. People just stared in disbelief at this unbelievable Cadillac limousine. Then we decided to head south on Market through Boardman and woke all them up. We then got on the Ohio Turnpike and drove out to the Howard Johnson's rest stop to get something to eat then back down Market St. raising hell. We thought Pantelas will never know as he lived in Warren and we didn't go anywhere near there. The next morning Geoff drives Tiny Tim and Miss Vicki to Hopkins Airport and returned the limo. On the way on the Ohio Turnpike, Geoff told Tiny how much fun it was to stand and put you head out the open roof. So, Tiny stood up as Geoff opened the roof and blasted the *Bridge On The River Kwai* and everybody on the turnpike blew their horns as they recognized Tiny Tim.

That night we were at the Apartment in Geoff's office and Pantelas walks in. He says 'You know I didn't go home last night. I just got a motel room in Boardman but I couldn't sleep. It was the strangest thing, I kept hearing that God damned *Bridge On The River Kwai* all night. He knew what we had done.

41

THE GREAT BOB MACK AND PITTSBURGH

The second year of Blue Ash and the first with Bill "Cupid' Bartolin started off with a bang.

We had our first recording session at Sigma Sound in Philadelphia with the famous Pittsburgh DJ, Bob Mack. Bob was also a well known teen dance promoter around Pittsburgh and was also the legendary discoverer of Tommy James in 1966. Bob started booking us as soon as Cupid joined the band in October of 1970. Bob had three teen clubs in the Pittsburgh area: The White Elephant in Irwin, The Tarena in Tarentum and The Lebanon Lodge in Mt. Lebanon. We'd play all three the same night. We'd play 20 minutes at each venue then tear down the equipment, travel to the next and tear down again. I asked Bob why we couldn't play all night at each place and he said 'That would just spoil them'. When we got to the Lebanon Lodge the stage area was roped off and I asked Bob why. He said 'I'm going to have bouncers too. When those rich girls from Mt. Lebanon and Upper St. Clair get a load of you guys they're going to tear you apart'. The first time we played there a girl got through and planted a big kiss on me while I was playing just like in the 'Birth Of The Beatles' movie. It was pretty cool as that had never happened before.

Bob took us to Sigma Sound Studio in Philadelphia to record twice. It was our first foray into a recording studio. Bob had a song called *We'll Live Tomorrow* which was a tribute to Jimi Hendrix and Janis Joplin who had just died. It was written by a girl from Pittsburgh named Teri Gruber. So we went to Philly to record. It wasn't a bad song and it was a great recording. While we were doing it, Wilson Pickett who was also recording in another studio there popped in and with his great smile and gave his opinion. 'You guys aren't bad... for white boys'. We all laughed. Bob tried to shop the recording around but couldn't get any interest which is funny now because when I listen to it today it could have been a major hit in 1971.

Throughout 1971 and 1972 we became very popular in Pittsburgh as Go Attractions from Shadyside with Rich Engler and Paul St. John were booking us as well. We were playing Pittsburgh 4 or 5 nights a week. We were regulars at the Bower Hill Community Church in Mt. Lebanon, The Psychedelia in McKees Rocks, The Luv

Inn on Forbes near Pitt, Murray's Speakeasy in New Brighton, The Electric Spider in McKeesport, Fontbonne Academy and Sewickley Academy as well as most of the high schools and colleges in Allegheny County as well as Bob's teen places. We were also branching out all over PA, NY, Ohio and W.Va. We'd go up once every month and play 4 dates in Upstate NY in Jamestown, Port Allegheny at the Spot and the Melody Inn at Busti. We were also regulars at the Penn Alto Ballroom in Altoona and the Holidaysburg YMCA and Weedville at the Valley Cave and La Hacienda in Milton PA and in Punxatawney (Yes, the Groundhog Day place) which we played over and over again. We also played Wheeling, Weirton and Follansbee W.Va quite a bit as well as Huntington at Marshall University where we ruled. We were scheduled to play with Badfinger in Huntington but it was canceled when in November of 1970 the whole Marshall football team was tragically killed in an airplane crash. That was such a tragedy. There's a movie about it called "We Are Marshall'" which is very moving.

In addition to playing practically every town in PA we also had our regular gigs in and around Youngstown Ohio and were also playing in Akron, Canton and Cleveland and Columbus. We also opened many a concert such as Cactus at the University of Pittsburgh, Bradford, Crazy Elephant at the Freak Out, David Cassidy at WHOT Hot Day at Idora Park, Youngstown as well opening there for Bobby Sherman as well. We played a week with the Box Tops over PA and Ohio. We were busy lads playing 250-275 gigs a year and were road tested and tight and armed with tons of original songs when we walked into Peppermint Productions of Youngstown that summer.

42

PEPPERMINT AND MERCURY

In June of 1972, we signed a production contract with Peppermint productions of Youngstown, Ohio. We started recording our first demos right away *Silver Horses, I Remember A Time, Abracadabra, You Don't Know What It's Like* and *Here We Go Again* with Gary Rhamy engineering and John Grazier producing. John also wrote a string quartet part for *Silver Horses* that he had the Kent State University String Quartet play on it. We had a very unique production deal with Peppermint in which we'd get 2 full days of recording for free every month for 5 years. After Peppermint set out our first demos we were very surprised to have 4 companies interested in us: Mercury, Polydor, MGM and Metromedia who had Bobby Sherman. That summer of 1972 famed rock critic and A&R man, Paul Nelson worked at Mercury Records. One particular day that summer there was a guy from Warren, Ohio named Gary Del Vecchio who was in Paul's office promoting his band. Gary recently told me he got a record deal for his band too at Mercury but it fell through cause they didn't have management. Anyway, that day there were stacks of demos all over Paul's office as dozens probably came every day in the morning mail. Gary saw our tape on top of one the stacks and told Paul he should listen to it and that we were very good. Paul put it on and was completely knocked out by the music. He called co-worker Bud Scoppa and Bud loved the tape too.

Here's where it even gets crazier. Paul and Bud went out to eat that night at their favorite restaurant in Manhattan called La Strada. At a table next to them were three girls from Jamestown, NY that had come to the city for a vacation. Suddenly, Paul and Bud heard the girls talking about Blue Ash--we played often in the Jamestown area--and Paul and Bud couldn't believe the coincidence. They asked the girls all about us and said they were from Mercury Records and had received a tape from Blue Ash and were thinking about signing them to a recording contract. The girls told them that we were really great live. Paul called Peppermint and Geoff Jones and said he was interested in seeing us perform and asked if we had any other recordings. Bill and I were so turned on we wrote *Plain To See* and *Day And Night* that night and recorded them the next day and Peppermint sent them to Paul who really loved them. Paul made arrangements with Geoff Jones our manager to fly down and see us in person. Geoff had booked us at the Apartment nite club in Youngstown where he had his office in the back and brought in Paul to meet us. We played our set and went back into Geoff's office. We waited 5, 10, 15 minutes and Paul didn't come back. Geoff said 'Maybe, he didn't like you guys'. Then, I said 'Well, I'm going to go out and talk to him'. He was sitting at the bar and I asked him, 'So, what did you think, Paul?' He said 'I think you guys are one of the best bands in America and I'm going to sign you to Mercury Records. I've been sitting out here trying to plan it all out'.

I went back to the office and said to the guys 'Pack your bags boys, we've just been called up to the major leagues'.

43

CUPID'S BACHELOR PARTY AND A DARK HAIRED GIRL IN PICCADILLY CIRCUS

When we had a bachelor party for Bill Bartolin in October of 1972, Bruce and Geoff Jones and I got the great idea to go to England the day after the wedding on Saturday, October 7th of 1972. This was the Wednesday before and we had no passports. We found only way you could get passports quickly was if someone you knew had died had overseas. So that was our story. Bruce's mom was involved in politics and pulled a lot of political strings and contacted our assemblyman. So we drove 300 miles to Harrisburg (the capital) of Pennsylvania and the Lt. Governor and a Assemblyman met us there and had all our papers and we had to then drive to Philadelphia to get our passports. That was the Thursday and Friday before the wedding then we drove back to Sharon in time for the Bill and Darla's wedding. Mind you we are going non-stop all the time. The next day after the wedding we drove to the Pittsburgh airport. We got on the plane and just passed out. About 8 hours later Bruce wakes up and looks at me and says 'Where in hell are we?' I said 'That's Ireland below us'. We landed a little while later at Heathrow around 8:00am. We checked into our hotel, The Royal Eagle by Hyde Park but Geoff and Bowie were beat and wanted to sleep a while and then we'd hit the town that night. Not me, I wanted to see a bit of London so I started walking and taking in the sights and doing some shopping. Around noon I ended up at Piccadilly Circus.

I bought an ice cream cone from a vendor there and was just standing and checking out that wonderful place. I was standing alone by the entrance of the tube station. Suddenly, I saw an extraordinary girl walk across the street and right toward me. She was very beautiful. She walked right up to me and bent over and took a bite out of my ice cream cone. Then she gave me this great smile and walked into the Underground Station. It was one of the most romantic and sexy things I have ever experienced. It lasted a whole twenty seconds and we never exchanged a word.

That was the craziest trip I was ever on. Bruce 'Bowie' McNeeledge and I decided to go to a different country for a few days. Geoff wanted to stay in London and do some filming. So we took the train from Victoria Station to Dover. At Dover we flipped a coin for France or Belgium. France won, so we bought ferry tickets to Boulogne-sur-Mer. The very same Boulogne-sur-Mer where in 1805, Napoleon Bonaparte massed his Grand Armee to invade England and left troops there as a feint and marched his army 500 miles in 40 days to fight the Russians and Austrians and win the greatest battle in the annals of military history (by most military scholars) at Austerlitz.

We were drinking Scotch and Coke on the ferry so when we landed in France we were pretty lit already. When we got off the boat we thought it was funny there was no customs station apparently we found out later we maybe had walked out with the crew. So we hit a few record stores in Boulogne and Bruce bought of ton of Rolling Stones EP's with great picture covers that we had never seen before, we also bought Cognac and I bought a lot of cartons of Gauloise and my fave Gitanes cigarettes.

Then we hit a bar in the harbor and were drinking and minding our own business and some French sailors started mouthing off and tried picking a fight with us at two o'clock in the afternoon. What assholes they were. I guess every country has them. They had on berets and striped shirts just like old movie stereotypes. We were out numbered about 5 to 1 so it was no use sticking around there. We got something to eat and headed back to the ferry station. We took the night ferry back to Dover and as we were very drunk and fell asleep as soon as we boarded. We were still asleep in Dover after all the passengers had already departed and all the lights were on and a couple of crew members shook us awake. Going through British customs the officer looked at out passports and asked 'Where have you gentlemen been?' I said 'France'. He said 'The stamp on your passports indicates you embarked from Britain but you didn't go anywhere and now you're coming back to Britain?' I said 'I don't know, here are our tickets we just walked off the boat in Boulogne with everyone else'. They let Bruce go through okay but took me to a back room and interrogated me for about an hour then made me pay a duty on my cigarettes. So, by the time we got out of there at midnight all the trains were done for the day. There was one cab and I asked where we could get a train to London. He said 'I could take you to Folkestone and there will be train going through there and you wait for the train and just pay them on board'. I said 'That's cool, let's do that'.

We get on at Folkestone and we had been drinking and not sleeping for maybe 36 hours. The standard fare from there to London was about a pound then. I gave the conductor a twenty pound note for both of us and there was some conversation but he must have misunderstood where we were going or just took us for a great piss-take. Anyway we both passed out and when we awoke there were tickets visibly stuck in our jacket pockets and it was eight hours later and we were somewhere far from London. We got off at the next stop where there was a quaint little rail station and a little guy in a British Railways uniform and a hundred sheep on the side of a green hill. We alighted the train and waited for the next one back to London.

The next night we went to the famous Speakeasy Club where all the rock stars hung out. We ended up in a little area where there was a bar and a few people there. At a table were Carmine Appice and Tim Bogert and a couple of girls. They had just started Beck, Bogert and Appice and there were posters about them all over London. Jeff Beck was there as well.

Blue Ash had just played with Cactus (Bogert, Appice, Day, McCarty) at the University of Pittsburgh, Bradford about 9 months before. I walked up to Carmine, 'Hi Carmine., I'm Frank from Blue Ash, we played with you guys a little while ago in Pennsylvania'. Nah man, Ya know... I meet so many people, I don't know man'. So we walked away and went over and sat at the bar next to two guys. One said, 'Are you Americans?' I said 'Yeah', 'Where are you from?', Youngstown, Ohio, you've probably never heard of it. Then one of them said 'Idora Park. That was one of the best gigs on our last tour'. Then they introduced themselves. It was Tommy Evans from Badfinger and some other guy. I told them how were supposed to play with them at Marshall University. Then Jeff Beck (who is probably the nicest man in Rock and Roll) came over and bought us beers. Later in the late 70's and early 80's, Stiv and I would run in to Jeff all the time in LA. He even invited us to a party which was really cool.

The reason Mr. Appice could not remember Blue Ash was that when we opened for Cactus we went over really well. Cactus came on late and they were all stoned and drunk out of their minds. The were so sloppy they couldn't even play let alone finish and stormed off the stage and had a big shouting match backstage as the crowd cheered "We Want Blue Ash!". I had never seen a band be that unprofessional in my life. It was always a mistake for a name act to not come with their A-Game if either Blue Ash or Raspberries were opening for them as we were consummate professionals. Blue Ash would never even think of drinking even one beer before we went on stage and we never did drugs. We just never did.

This would not be the last time Blue Ash would meet up with Mr. Appice and Bogert. We shared the same bill with them again with them as Vanilla Fudge in 2004 when we did our reunion gig at the B & B Backstage in Youngstown in 2004. More on that later. Anyway, our trip to England was a great fun trip because we knew when we returned to America, Paul Nelson and Bud Scoppa were coming down from New York and we would start selecting songs for our debut album on Mercury Records.

A DARK-HAIRED GIRL IN PICCADILLY CIRCUS

(Frank Secich)

A dark-haired girl in Piccadilly once
Made quite an impression on me
She crossed the street without ever looking up
Eating chips from a paper cup

A dark-haired girl in Piccadilly walked
Right to where I was alone
Then moved in closer & without a word
Took a bite of my ice cream cone

Then she smiled & walked away
Disappeared into the underground & went in
Down by a sign that read the Bakerloo Line

I stood for a bus wanting the action of a train
I lit a Gitanes it began to rain
I hailed a taxi with a Daily Mail
The driver said "Where to mate?

Among the placards on the square
My eyes drifted toward
A poster advertising "Young Winston" starring Simon Ward

I said "let's drive around this Circus for a while"
He tipped his hat began to smile
Then we'll drop me off at my hotel on Craven Road
It's the Royal Eagle you should know it well

The Dark-Haired girl in Piccadilly & I
Never spoke on that overcast day
I went home & she went by the by
Just once I'd love to see her again
I'd ask her, her name

44

RECORDING "NO MORE NO LESS" AT PEPPERMINT FEBRUARY, MARCH 1973

We signed with Mercury Records in December of 1972 and started recording or debut album "No More, No Less" at Peppermint Productions in Youngstown, Ohio on February 1st. We had John Grazier producing and Gary Rhamy who owned Peppermint was the engineer. We were in good hands. We recorded all of February on the week days and played out live on the weekends and in March mixed for two weeks. Paul Nelson was also on hand for all the sessions and would commute by plane to NY on the weekends.

We recorded 16 songs all together and picked 12 for "No More, No Less", *Abracadabra (Have You Seen Her?), Dusty Old Fairgrounds, Plain to See, Just Another Game, I Remember a Time, Smash My Guitar, Any Time At All, Here We Go Again, What Can I Do for You?, All I Want, Wasting My Time* and *Let There Be Rock*. Four songs didn't make the cut, *Oh No Not Again, Northern Comforts, She Cried for 15 Years* and *It's All In Your Mind*.

Paul Nelson had given us a bootleg of Bob Dylan's 'Dusty Old Fairgrounds' and asked if we wanted to record it. We were huge Dylan fans and jumped at the chance. Bill Bartolin rearranged and we gave it The Who' treatment. So when Mercury was preparing the album release they had to get a clearance from Bob Dylan's publishing company, Warner Brothers. Warner Brothers had never heard of it so they played it for Dylan and he said he liked it and that he did write the song. He told his publisher to tell Mercury to put it on a single because it would get a lot of attention which they did and it did. Paul Nelson was an old friend of Dylan's from Minnesota and was featured in Martin Scorsese's film No Direction Home. Paul was also known for his legendary rock writing and interviews in Rolling Stone and many others. There's great book out about him by Kevin Avery called "Everything Is an Afterthought (The Life And Writings Of Paul Nelson)". We finished the album at 5:00 am in the morning on the last day with the ritual of me smashing a guitar on a large grey brick surrounded by very expensive microphones. I did it on one take to put the finishing touches on our song *Smash My Guitar*. After we had finished mixing the LP we invited our old pal and mentor Boots Bell down to Peppermint to listen. He gave us his blessing so everything was alright.

ABRACADABRA (Have You Seen Her?)

(Secich-Bartolin)

Have you seen her?
Have you seen her?

There must be magic in the air
First she's here and then she's there
Now you see her, now you don't
First she'll do you then she won't

Have you seen her?
Have you seen her?

I was young and I was green
She was old and she was mean
A fortune telling queen
Like nothing I'd never seen

Have you seen her?
Have you seen her?

Such a magical lady
I let her cry on my shoulder
Slightly tragical maybe
Now she's getting older
She keeps getting older

Have you seen her?
Have you seen her?

I'll pull a rabbit out my hat
And offer it to you
But I don't know where you're at
Or who to send it to

Have you seen her?
Have you seen her?

She resorts to using tricks
People say that she's quite slick
Well I know and just the same
I think Houdini is to blame

Have you seen her?
Have you seen her?

Such a magical lady
I let her cry on my shoulder
Slightly tragical maybe
Now she's getting older
She keeps getting older

Have you seen her?

45

ALMOST FAMOUS THE FIRST TIME – 1973

We became a big hit with the rock press even before our record was released. Critical Darlings the press called us along with Badfinger, Raspberries and Big Star. While we were recording Gary Kenton from Creem Magazine came down to Youngstown to hang out with us and wrote a two-page article in Creem that came out a few weeks before the album was released. Greg Shaw got in touch with us after he received an advance demo copy of the album. Greg was then editor of Phonograph Record Magazine which was second only to Rolling Stone in the rock press world and had his own radio show in LA and was raving mad about us. Our debut LP "No More, No Less" was released in mid-May and the critical accolades came pouring in:

"No More No Less is an astonishingly explosive debut, and with apparently limitless potential, Blue Ash should by all rights become a major phenomenon" **Ken Barnes- Rolling Stone**

"I wish, I wish, I wish. There's this song, I Remember A Time, on Blue Ash's debut album It could do for this group what Mr. Tambourine Man did for the Byrds: the start of a brilliant career, a Number One hit, instant mythology." **Mike Saunders- Phonograph Record Magazine**

"Musically the four-man group attacks like a shock wave. The LP is without a doubt one of the finest debut albums of the rock era." **Dave Goeller-Army Times**

"Their easy going songs are much like those of the Dave Clark Five or The Beatles before Sgt. Pepper--a return to good, melodic, dance able rock 'n' roll". says **Thom Hansard- Houston Chronicle**

"Where are all the great rock 'n' roll bands coming from these days? England? New York? San Francisco? Nope It's Youngstown, Ohio" **Gary Kenton- Creem**

We had hundreds more just like these coming in from all over the country and Canada. Our future seemed very good and wide open.

In May of 1973, Me, Paul Nelson and John Grazier went to Cleveland with the album to take it to the radio stations. Denny Sanders was "live" on the air at WMMS. He was playing a Led Zeppelin LP. Outside of Denny's glass enclosure Paul held up the album. Denny motions for us to come on in. He pulls the needle right over the Zeppelin album and says 'Hey, Blue Ash just rolled in with their new LP and we're going to give it a listen'. So, he plays the first two songs *Abracadabra* and *Dusty Old Fairgrounds* without even listening to them first. Then on the air he said 'This album is great!' They put us right into heavy rotation. It used to be a much cooler world back then. Kid Leo who was also DJ at WMMS used to play the hell out of us as well and we played at Fat Glenn's at CSU and the Atomic Alps regularly.

46

SUNGLASS CITY

Whenever Blue Ash would hit New York City, Sunglass City would be one of our first stops. It was located right at Times Square where the arcade used to be. They had the greatest sunglasses in the world and we always bought some there. In the movie Fail Safe as they count down from 10 to 1 as the A bomb is dropped on the Big Apple it freeze frames at one on Times Square right where Sunglass City was located.

That always struck me funny so I wrote a song about it.

SUNGLASS CITY

(Frank Secich)

I'm going to Sun Glass City
For the end of the world
I'm going to get smashed & celebrate with my girl
Then we're going to stay overnight at the Hotel Earle

I'm walking 'round Sun Glass City
Hey! there's Johnny Burnette
Outside of Bleecker Bob's with Lester Bangs
They blew into Sun Glass City
Like the Dalton Gang

Through a revolving door
Into a mercury mirror
That was once the floor
That ricocheted the tears back into my eyes

I'm going Sun Glass City then
Max's Kansas City
Where the girls are pretty, cold & cruel
I'm going to Sun Glass City as fast as a fool

I'm stumbling around Sun Glass City
In a maze of twists and turns
I had some real concerns for a while
Is Paris burning or is just the world on fire?

Run down the subway stairs
Onto a ceramic platform
Into the underground
See the windows through the faces
Waiting by the train

I'm going to Sun Glass City
I'll be the last man crawling
Around the Chelsea Hotel in 2012
I'm going to Sun Glass City
I guess I'll see you there too

47

OUR 2ND SINGLE RELEASE – JULY 1973

On June 15, 1973 Blue Ash flew to Chicago to play the Aragon Ballroom with Iggy & The Stooges and Detroit with Mitch Ryder. We also spent the day at Mercury Records on Wacker Drive meeting all the execs and people who worked there. We were touring and playing everywhere that summer promoting "No More, No Less".

In mid-summer of 1973 Mercury released our second single *I Remember A Time* b/w *Plain To See* which was I thought was a great double single. It got good radio and sold well in some cities like Cincinnati and Boston but failed to become a national hit. Today of course it's a well sought after collector's item.

Paul Nelson would always go see Rod Stewart as Mercury's representative and more so as his friend whenever Rod was in the east in New York. New Jersey or Boston. Paul told me he was making a trip to Boston where Rod was playing and that he was going to give Rod a "No More, No Less" LP. Months later, I remembered that and asked Paul if Rod had ever said anything about the Blue Ash album. Paul said 'Yeah, he really liked it and especially liked *I Remember A Time*'. I thought that was so cool and such a great compliment.

I REMEMBER A TIME

(Secich-Bartolin)

I remember the days
When we were young
I remember the days
When we were one
Do you, do you, do you
Do you recall
I'm just looking back
At times we had both good and bad
I remember all things we planned

I remember, I remember, I remember
I'll remember those days all my life

I remember a time
When nothing mattered
(I remember the time)
Do you remember the time
We got caught by the cops
(I remember the time)
Do you, do you, do you
Do you recall
I'm just looking back
At times we had both good and bad
I remember all things we planned

I remember, I remember, I remember
I'll remember those days all my life

I'll remember what we said
How can I forget
I'll remember all the things we did
And I'll have no regrets

I remember, I remember, I remember
I'll remember, I'll remember
You all the days of my life

48

YOKO ONO – OCTOBER 1973

We met Yoko in October of 1973. I believe John had gone off on his lost weekend to Los Angeles a few weeks before. Anyway, Yoko was playing her solo material at a club in New York called Kenny's Castaway's. Jim Kendzor, Geoff Jones and I were in New York doing Mercury Records business.

We were just about to leave when I picked up a Village Voice and saw that Yoko was appearing that night. That was the only advertisement and the only time she ever did that. We decided to go the show. When we got there it was sold out and we couldn't get in. David Johansen and Elliott Murphy both came by and we all stood on the sidewalk talking. Just then a guy who worked for Yoko came out to have a cigarette. He recognized us and he was a big Blue Ash fan. He got us in then after the show took us back stage to meet Yoko. Andy Warhol was there as well. Yoko was a great lady and very friendly. Geoff gave her a Blue Ash album. She asked Jim and I if we would autograph the album for her which blew our minds. Bob Gruen, who was her photographer took some pictures and they ended up in dozens of magazines including Rolling Stone. The picture you see in this book was taken by our manager Geoff Jones at the same time.

49

RASPBERRIES AND BLUE ASH - PACKARD MUSIC HALL - JANUARY 31 1974

Now here was a Powerpop Dream Concert if there ever was one with both Raspberries and Blue Ash in our primes. There has been a great bootleg of this concert floating around for 40 years. It was recorded by my friend Mike Greenfield on a cassette machine in the audience. Paul Nelson had also flown down from New York to attend this classic concert. The Raspberries and Blue Ash played in front of 3,000 crazy kids that night. I don't think either band ever sounded better. It was the first time that I'd heard the Raspberries with the mellotrons. It was great. This was the Raspberries line-up with Eric Carmen, Wally Bryson, Scott McCarl and Mike McBride on drums which was 3/4's (Eric, Wally and Mike) of the classic Cyrus Erie line-up 1968-69. The Cyrus Erie line-up of Eric Wally and the McBride brothers in my opinion may just have been the best 'live' American group of all time. So, this new Raspberries came very close to that personnel wise.

They just killed. Blue Ash did our high energy set opening with blistering version of Chan Romero's *Hippy, Hippy Shake* then burned through a lot our songs from "No More, No Less" throwing in a cover of the Contours *Do You Love Me?* and the Isley's *Twist and Shout* and finally ending with crazy version of *My Generation*. I'd like to include this on the big boxed set of Blue Ash coming from Australia on Zero Hour in 2016. That night was my favorite concert I ever played with Blue Ash.... Until we played with the Stooges in Detroit ten days later.

50

METALLIC KO AT THE MICHIGAN PALACE – FEBRUARY 9 1974

On February 9, 1974 exactly ten years from the day the Beatles debuted in America on the Ed Sullivan Show, Blue Ash played with the Stooges at their final show before they broke up at the Michigan Palace in Detroit. The Palace had a seating capacity of 4,038. It was a great place to play and it was packed. There was another band on before us and they came bolting off the stage saying don't go out there, It's crazy! Undaunted as we always were, Blue Ash took the stage and had one of our best concerts ever. We sounded cool and went over great. We had a lot of fans in Detroit and always sold a lot of records there.

The Stooges were up next and there was a sinister, foreboding feeling in the air. As we were changing gear between bands we left one of our guitars (Jim's Epiphone Sheraton) on stage on a guitar stand. We stood on the side of the stage to get a good view of the show. Iggy was in rare form that night even for him and you just knew it was coming. After the opening song, *"Ow! Ow! Riots in the Motor City! Kind ladies and gentlemen the Stooges next presentation this evening will be for all you boys and girls who want to slow dance. It's called "I Got Shit!"* He was literally egging on the crowd on so to speak with *I Got Nothin*. Eggs, beer bottles, ice, jelly beans and all kind of debris were flying at the stage. *"Our next selection tonight for all you Hebrew ladies in the audience is entitled Rich Bitch. Hey, I don't care if you throw all the ice in the world, you're paying 5 bucks and I'm making $10,000 baby"*. Then the intro to *Gimme Danger*. *"What do you want to hear? Say, you wanna hear, Louie, Louie? Where Did Our Love Go?* Then in falsetto *"Baby baby, where did my cock go?"* After *"Gimme Danger"* the automatic self-destruction of a legendary band continues in high gear. *"Well, well ladies and gentlemen. Thank you for your kind indulgence and for this evening's next selection I'll be proud to present a song that was co-written by my mother entitled "I Got My Cock In My Pocket"* and a one, and a two fuck you pricks!* Then after one more rambling soliloquy they broke into as promised *Louie Louie* and all hell breaks loose *"I never thought it would come to this baby"*.

We were on the side of the stage laughing our asses off and falling about in hysterics it was so funny. Then after the fall apart *Louie, Louie* ending. *"Thank you very much to the person who threw this glass bottle at my head and nearly killed me. You missed again, keep trying next week."*

At the end when we retrieved our stage guitar and there was yellow egg splatter all over it. Jim left it on there and never cleaned it and just let it dry on there. It was a souvenir of an historic night. Jim still owns that guitar and I'll bet the egg splatter is still on it. The Stooges would not play together again for another 29 years until they reunited in 2003.

51

THE JOINT IN THE WOODS AND AMERICAN BANDSTAND

We got booked in April of 1974 by our booking agency ABC into the Joint In The Woods in Parsippany, New Jersey. It was supposed to be the biggest nite club in the Eastern U.S. It held some thing like 2000 people. So, every night we would open for a famous act. I think the first night was Nazareth, then Marshall Tucker Band, then Lloyd Price. Those gigs all went great and we went over very well. The last night was opening for Commander Cody and His Lost Planet Airmen of *Hot Rod Lincoln* fame. The crowd that night was way different than the previous nights. The place was filled drunken rednecks who were in no mood for the power pop of Blue Ash. It was the only night ever in Blue Ash's history of over 1400 gigs did we ever get booed and things thrown at us. We kept playing and it just got worse but we weren't going to be thrown off a stage by a bunch of drunken redneck hillbillies. As about the tenth beer bottle was thrown at us, Jim Kendzor did one of the greatest things ever on stage. He caught the bottle in mid-air and threw it like a fastball right back into the crowd. It was funny because once he did that the heckling and throwing stopped. After the song we just said 'Throw any more and they're coming right back at you'.

What a weird night. What made it even funnier was that afternoon at the motel before the gig we were watching American Bandstand and Dick Clark says 'Right after this break we'll be back with Rate-A-Record and we have two great ones'. I told Jim 'I hate that Rate -A- Record shit and slammed the off button on the TV. Then all afternoon we got calls from everyone: Our mothers, friends , fans and at the gig that night everyone was coming up to us. Hey! You guys were on American Bandstand today with *Anytime At All* (our new single on Mercury) and got a 95 and Dick Clark really talked it up big time.

52

MERCURY POISONING....

When "No More, No Less" was released as I had mentioned earlier we got rave reviews in all the rock press Rolling Stone, Creem, Crawdaddy, Phonograph Record Magazine, Billboard, Rock Scene, Zoo World, The Real Paper, Record World, Cash Box and tons of big dailies around the country. We got great radio airplay in markets like Boston, Detroit, Cleveland and Miami but we couldn't crack the New York and LA markets. Mercury made two pressings of 10,000 each and we sold 19,500 and we had to sell 25,000 with our contract to get a second album. When we fell short of that goal the troubles started with the suits in the company.

Paul Nelson and Bud Scoppa and all the A&R guys at the company in New York and Chicago fought for us to the very end. Our problem was with the promotion men at the company who hated us. The food chain at Mercury at that time went something like this: Rod Stewart, BTO, The New York Dolls and lastly Blue Ash. One time the famous syndicated columnist Bob Greene from the Chicago Tribune wanted to do a big article on us for New Times magazine. He called to set it up and they actually said to him 'Why don't you do an article on Rod Stewart or BTO instead?' He said 'I'm doing one on Blue Ash', which he did and really slammed them for their treatment of us. I'm sure the New Times article didn't go over well with the suits but that's what we were dealing with there. It's was decided to give us one more single *Anytime At All* b/w *She's So Nice* and if that didn't hit we would be dropped. It didn't and we were. Even Dick Clark championed us but the promo department just didn't care.

We continued to play everywhere but around that time David Evans left the band and Jeff Rozniata who was our roadie stepped in on drums for the next two years. We had a lot of interest from other labels. Columbia Records flew the band up to New York and we auditioned for almost the entire company in their famous Studio A. They would bring in 20 people at a time and we would play a few songs for each group. We thought we did well but something happened and we didn't get signed. Next was RCA and almost the same thing. Then Nat Weiss who owned Nemperor Records and was the Beatles' American lawyer and Brian Epstein's good friend came to Youngstown for a couple of days to hang out with us and we played live in Peppermint Studios for him. He loved the band but just like the others at the last minute something would fall through. It's a tough business and we were really getting frustrated but we continued to play out adding in 1976 another guitar, Max Schang, keyboards, Brian Wingrove and drums, George Grexa.

53

MEETING LISA IN BUHL PARK – JULY 3 1974

I talked earlier in the book about meeting my first love and muse. Eight years later on almost the same exact spot in Buhl Park I met the love of my life, Lisa Tidmarsh. Blue Ash had a rare week off for the holiday and I was trying to book a last minute flight to Nova Scotia to go on vacation but wasn't having any luck as most flights over the July 4th holiday were well booked. So, I decided to just take a drive up to Buhl Park and take a walk and try to leave the next day. I parked across from the ball field inside the Buhl Blvd. entrance. Ahead of me in a dark green Fiat convertible were three girls. The other two were Lisa's cousin Paula (Komar) Heath and her friend Beth (Madura) Kleja. They got out and started walking toward the lake. I got out and walked the same way behind them. I thought if that blonde on the end looks anything near how she looks from the back then I've got to meet her. So I sped up and passed them on the outside and said hello to the blonde and she said hi and I just kept walking.

I later went back to my car and just sat on the hood smoking a cigarette. They came back to the Fiat and the blonde walked over to me and with a cigarette and asked me for a light saying her lighter didn't work. So I gave her a light and we started talking. I found out a little later that she didn't even smoke. The next night we got together and she drove me around in her Fiat Convertible and we had a great time and in the evening. I kissed her for the first time and the fireworks went off. I mean literally went off, like it was right on cue. It was the Fourth of July. We went together for the next 3 years and got married on October 8, 1977. Even more than my wife, Lisa's my best friend and soul mate and muse. We've had a million laughs and good times together. We've been together for 41 years so I think we're going to last.

54

CRAZY ASS

In August of 1974, Blue Ash got booked by the famous concert promoter Bill Graham to play a concert for AIM in Hayward, Wisconsin. It was mainly Native American acts but we were brought in to close the show in the late afternoon for the kids. They put us up at a great place called the Telemark Lodge. On the bill were many Native American activists, musicians and artists such as Dennis Banks and Russell Means (later also stars of The Last Of The Mohicans), Sacheen Little Feather (who had recently refused Marlon Brando's Oscar and gave her famous speech at the Oscar ceremonies), Buffy Ste. Marie was performing as well. She was always one of my heroes especially for writing *Universal Soldier* which is one of my favorite songs and it was so great for me to meet her. It was also a big get together for the Lakota Sioux and a Pow Wow the next day. The concert was held in a stadium that surrounded a small lake that I had already been familiar with it because ABC's Wide World Of Sports and others always had competitions for lumberjacks and outdoorsmen there. The stage was in the middle of the lake and electrical cables were wired in the air out to it and we had to be rowed out there. It was very different to say the least.

As we took the stage there was a lot of excitement in the air. The kids were absolutely going crazy and bonkers over us. We built up great momentum and as we went into our last song we were wildly jumping about the stage when I crashed right into the big Ampeg bass amp they had provided for me. As I saw it start to teeter and fall into the lake, I threw my Gibson bass guitar high in the air as I did not want to be electrocuted. As the bass was airborne it pulled the cable out of the amp and I caught it coming down as I watched the amp slowly sink into the lake. I looked toward shore and could see our manager Geoff Jones just shaking his head. He knew my stunt would cost me probably a couple thousand dollars in damages. Anyway, the kids went absolutely nuts and cheered and cheered and cheered. After we were taken off the stage we were mobbed and we stayed there and signed autographs and took photos with the kids for a couple of hours.

When we were done, Geoff got out his checkbook and he and I went in to settle up with the promoter and the Native Americans who were running the event. We went inside a building and there at a table were Bill Graham, Russell Means and Dennis

Banks sitting. Geoff says 'Okay, sorry Bill how much do we owe you for the damaged amp?' Then Bill Graham said 'Put away your checkbook, Geoff, that was a great concert and we'll get it fixed'. Then he paid us and I was very relieved. Then I can't remember which one but either Dennis or Russell said 'You know we've come up with an Indian name for you'. I asked apprehensively 'What's that?' And he said 'Crazy Ass' and we all busted up laughing. Then they said they were amazed not only by our show but even more by the fact that we hung out later and talked to all the kids signing autographs, taking photos with them, joking around with them and that really impressed them. They invited us to the Big Pow Wow the next day.

It was fantastic to be there on the windswept Northern plains on a cool August night with all those beautiful people sharing their music, food, rituals, stories and rich heritage. It made quite an impression on all of us.

55

PRINCE CARLTON, PRINCE TRACTION AND PRINCE DUDE

One time that May we were playing at the Voyager Inn in downtown Youngstown for an after prom for one of the local high schools. It was Woodrow Wilson High School I think. We often took jobs like that cause they paid very well and they didn't start until midnight and we could play another gig somewhere before. So we were playing for the kids in an upstairs ballroom they had for such occasions.

We didn't know it but Parliament/Funkedelic were staying at the Inn as they had a big concert earlier at Stambaugh Auditorium. When they got back to the hotel they heard a band upstairs playing late and crashed the party much to the delight of the kids and us and they hung out all night. They had a Canadian manager named Ron Scribner who was a great guy. He said to Geoff, 'Have you guys ever played in Canada?' Geoff said 'No', He said 'You guys would go over great there and I can book you some great gigs'. About a month later Ron called Geoff and had some great gigs for us. The first was a week's residency at Larry's Hideaway in Toronto which was in the bottom of the Prince Carlton Hotel. The hotel sat alone as a building in a park right across from Maple Leaf Gardens on Carlton St. We each had a free room at the hotel for the week and free food. There were three elderly gentlemen who worked eight hour shifts at the hotel desk through the day and night and they were real characters and would take care of us. We nicknamed them Prince Carlton, Prince Traction and Prince Dude. Larry's Hideaway was one of the coolest places Blue Ash ever played. We played 7 days there and the lines to get in went around half the block. If someone would leave the club they could not get back in and another person in the line would be let in. We were surprised and stunned at how well we went over there and we were really sounding our best. We met some great fans there like Crazy Pete who brought 2 cases of beer every night and Robert Lawrence who interviewed us on radio there. In addition to giving us free rooms in the hotel and food and drink every day the club paid very well. The best part was when we finished and got paid the owner gave me an envelope. In it were 4 crisp $100.00 Canadian bills. He said 'I had a great week with Blue Ash so give a bill to each guy in the group as a tip'. That was the first time that ever happened. It was a very cool place to play.

I would later play at this great club again in 1980 with the Dead Boys which I will describe in great detail in my series of Dead Boys vignettes later in the book. Then after going home for a week we came back up to Toronto and played Yonge Station for seven days which again was great. They wanted us to tour all over Canada that winter starting in Quebec but we had other obligations that winter. It's funny, Canada has always been a special place for us and myself. Blue Ash's reissue of "No More, No Less" on CD hit Number 1 on Amazon Canada's power pop charts for 3 weeks 2008 and even broke the Top 200 of the entire country in any genre.

56

ROCKIN AT THE MOCCASIN BAR

Since we had gone over so well at Native American concert at the end of summer, we were booked by the Telemark Lodge in Hayward, Wisconsin to play the whole week from the day after Christmas through New Years. We arrived a little early and our rooms weren't ready yet so the lodge got us rooms in town for one night then we'd have the rest of the week at the Lodge. They invited all of us up to the ski lodge and spa and said we could use all the facilities, skiing, saunas, food and drinks all the great stuff at this luxury spa. So Jim and Jeff and our roadies Steve and Roger went to the lodge to partake in all the amenities. Cupid and I were tired and stayed at the motel and were just going to go out in the town and get a sandwich and some beers. It was snowing like hell and you couldn't even see. We asked the desk clerk where the nearest tavern was and he pointed to the Moccasin Bar a few blocks away. We walked out of the snow and into the Moccasin Bar and it was packed to the gills. I mean literally. There were stuffed Muskie and Northern Pike trophy fish mounted on the walls and various deer and bear heads as well and people crammed inside wall to wall of all ages.

There was a great little band from Chicago playing with a cute girl guitarist. Cupid and I finally made it through the crowd to a space at the bar. A guy waited on us and I said 'Could we have a couple steak sandwiches and a couple of draughts?' Suddenly he said 'Are you guys, Blue Ash?,' I said 'Yeah', he said 'Put away your money guys. It's no good here. Whatever you want is on the house'. Apparently he was the owner of the establishment. Soon he brought us out food and drink as we settled in and watched the band who were really good. When the band took a break he brought them over and introduced us and asked 'Would you guys like to get up and do a number? The band would be honored and so would I and the crowd will go nuts'. So Cupid and I said 'Sure, why not'. I played bass and Cupid took the lead and the others backed. The owner introduced us and the crowd cheered wildly 'The guys from Blue Ash who played here last summer and will be at the Telemark all week are going to play a few numbers here tonight'. We broke right into *Slow Down*, the old Larry Williams song. We figured we'd just do old standards because the band would know the songs. We went into more like *Twist And Shout, Rock And Roll Music, Roll Over Beethoven* most with me singing and or members of the band taking a turn at vocals. We ended up playing the rest of the night to the wild appreciative crowd. Finally after hours of this the bar closed and Cupid and I walked back through the still snowing snowstorm to the motel and just collapsed. It was funny because we would later joke the it was one of our best nights ever playing and it wasn't even our band. It's one of my fondest memories..

57

PLAYBOY TIME

We continued to record demos every month at Peppermint so we had an enormous amount of material. In 1976 after all these disappointments, Jeff Rozniata left the band to move to California. Right after that we signed a production contract with Steve Friedman who used to work for Peppermint and Steve got us a singles contract with Playboy Records. We went to Criteria Recording Studio in Miami and recorded four songs. *Look At You Now* was picked as the first single and did very well. It was a regional hit all over the south: Texas, Oklahoma, Missouri, Arkansas, Mississippi, Louisiana and in Pennsylvania, Ohio and West Virginia. Hitting Top 40 on most stations and even number one in a few markets.

Playboy then offered us an LP deal. We flew to LA and finished the LP at Village Recorder in August of 1977 and Playboy released the 'Front Page News' album in October. A few months after the release Playboy International Records folded. 'Front Page News' did much better than "No More, No Less" selling 50,000 but again we were left in the cold. We would continue to record with Bobby Tocco on drums and Brian Wingrove on piano until January 1979. At the end of the decade, Bob Greene, the syndicated columnist from the Chicago Tribune wrote a column called "Bob Greene Presents The Best Of The 70's" wherein he listed the best books, movies, actors, actresses, TV Series, newspapers, magazines, plays, writers etc of the much maligned decade. He then listed Best English Band: The Who, then Best American Band: Blue Ash.

A bar band from Youngstown, Ohio, Blue Ash astonished critics with their 1973 debut album, "No More, No Less". Enlightened music writers across the country predicted that Blue Ash would be the next international phenomenon. They were never heard from again. After ten years together and after playing over 1400 gigs, Blue Ash called it quits. In 25 years we'd be back.

58

MY HONEYMOON WITH THE DEAD BOYS – OCTOBER 1977

Lisa and I were married in Hermitage, PA on October 8, 1977. Beaver Warner, Jim Kendzor, Geoff Jones and Bill Bartolin were all in our wedding party as well as Lisa's cousin, Paula Heath, my sister Maryann Secich Hartmann and Beth (Madura) Kleja. I wrote the song *It's So Easy* for Lisa and our wedding, Jim, Brain and Cupid performed it at the ceremony. Stiv was supposed to attend but at the last minute he had obligations with the Dead Boys who's initial album 'Young, Loud and Snotty' had just been released on Sire Records.

Lisa and I went on our honeymoon to Toronto and after we were there about a week, we met up with Brian Wingrove and his wife, Vickie. One afternoon Vickie and Lisa wanted to go shopping and Brian and I decided to make the rounds of the bars and record stores on Yonge Street. As we're passing by the New Yorker Theater, we see Stiv Bators walking out (I didn't even know the Dead Boys were in Canada, let alone playing there that night). They must have been doing a sound check in the afternoon. Stiv doesn't see us, so we walk behind him along Yonge Street and I start in with my best Canadian accent 'Hey Brian, will ya get a load of this guy? eh!' Then Brian says 'Looks like some fookin' American asshole to me...' Stiv still doesn't look around, so we keep following him and taking the piss out of him for about a whole block. Finally, I start laughing and say 'Hey Stiv! Turn around!' He does and then very calmly says 'I knew it was you guys all along' (like it wasn't the slightest bit strange that we randomly run into each other in another country) and I said 'You did NOT! We got you good!' And we all fell about laughing. We all went to the concert that night and had a great time... saw The Viletones who opened up as well.

59

ALMOST FAMOUS THE SECOND TIME (OVERVIEW 1979-81)
STIV BATORS TO THE RESCUE

These are the liner notes Greg Shaw asked me to write for the two Stiv Bators reissues 'Disconnected' and 'LA Confidential' that he was putting out in 2004 right before he passed away. I'd like to reprint them here as they will give you an idea of what we were up to in the years of 1979-80. Thanks so much to Suzy Shaw for letting me share them. I had such a great time working with Greg on this in the last 6 months of his life. It's one of my fondest memories - RIP Greg, Thom and Stiv.

Stiv and I loved everyone so much at Bomp! Greg, Suzy, Merle, Paul Grant and Rich Schmidt and we used to play great pranks on them. We'd go to the all night newsstand that was about a block long on Fairfax right near Canter's all night Deli in LA. Those newsstand guys were great. They'd even get me the Sharon Herald out there a few days late for a couple of bucks. Anyway, for an hour we'd rip the subscription cards out of every magazine then the all next day fill them all out in the names of the people at Bomp! Then we'd send them off in the mail. Paul Grant got me good though. He sent some records to my apartment COD and my elderly neighbor lady paid for them when I wasn't home. She thought it was something important for me. So, I paid her and thanked her. Paul got me good.

IT'S COLD OUTSIDE AND THE DISCONNECTED LP

Calling On You

On the first day of February of 1979, I received a telephone call from my old friend Stiv. 'Hey, you've got to come to California tomorrow morning!' I said, 'Stiv, it's 8:30 at night and I do have a job which I tend to go to every day'. Stiv went on... 'Seriously, there's a pre-paid ticket waiting for you at the Youngstown airport. I met this guy from Holland, who's an eccentric millionaire and he wants to put a tour together with all these punk groups and there's a lot of money in it. We have an entire floor at the Sunset Marquis'. I asked 'What kind of tour?' 'Just come out for a week, check it out. You will not believe what's going on here'. I said, 'I want at least $400 a week plus expenses'. 'Frank, you'll make that a day'.

The next morning I was on my way to Los Angeles, Stiv met me at LAX and we drove to the Sunset Marquis. He was right. The entire hotel seemed like a non-stop party. Stiv introduced me to our benefactor whom he referred to as 'Napoleon Blownapart' (for his physical appearance as much as for his chemical inclinations). He was a great guy. His idea was to put together a tour that would stop at random cities unannounced, pass out flyers and have spontaneous concerts. We would play and record 'live' on the spot via 200 high-speed duplicators and give out free recordings to all who attended. Using 'name' punk artists, word would spread of the happenings. We would have events everywhere. He was very excited at the prospects and had the money to do it. Apparently, he was a wealthy businessman in Europe and at age 40 decided to cash it in and come to LA for some fun. He passed out money like Terry Southern's 'Magic Christian' Guy Grand. The truth was he was a Jay Gatsby character and no one knew the truth about him. Many punk luminaries had already been recruited. Among them, Stiv, Joan Jett, Angie Bowie, Ben Brierley (who later that year married Marianne Faithfull) of Great Britain's 'Vibrators' and 'Pure Hell' (an all-black punk group from Philadelphia). Levi and the Rockats were there and Cheetah Chrome and Gyda Gash were coming, plus there were 5 or 6 pretty Dutch and French girls who worked for him and more people being recruited every day. I got to meet Greg Shaw there. He had helped my old band Blue Ash a lot when he was the editor of Phonograph Record Magazine. A film crew was coming from England.

It was a great time, but there was no organization or plan as far as I could tell. Stiv and I were there for the ride. No rehearsals or jams at all. After a few weeks, our tour director rented a dozen Winnebagos and parked them in a warehouse in Alhambra and from there we set off in a caravan to Ridgecrest, California.

Been To The Desert In A Winnebago With No Name

For fine tuning purposes before we hit the road, the tour had rented camping space at the fairgrounds in Ridgecrest. The Winnebagos were symbolically parked in a circle. On the surface it was a good choice because Ridgecrest was sadly lacking in the delights and distractions of Hollywood and we could get serious and start rehearsing. It didn't happen. The musicians would just hang out in the town every day. The local constabulary started harassing us and the citizenry were becoming agitated. There was a sinister feeling in the air and Stiv would remind me every day we were only a few miles from the Spahn ranch of Charlie Manson fame.

Confrontations with the locals were now a daily occurrence. We were written about in the local paper. Paranoia ran deep. Desertions started and discontent and mutiny were festering. Salaries were cut and we were put on a strict regimen. For the first time it started to suck. In the midst of all this Stiv and I decided to take a trip (as it were) to the Mojave desert a la Jim Morrison. We went to the top of a mountain. It was the most beautiful sight we had ever seen and dead quiet. We were a million miles away from the streets of Youngstown. We sat there for a long time taking it all in. Suddenly all hell broke loose. Bombs and explosions and fires were everywhere. Then it stopped. We found out later from the locals that we were looking out on the U.S. Naval Ordinance Testing Area. I guess we weren't that far from Ohio at all.

After a few days, Stiv and I returned back to earth, then the compound, which by now was almost deserted save for Eddy Best, Rick Bremmer and Pure Hell. Blown-apart's world and dream were coming undone, but our great leader was determined to have the final say. He piled all of the musical equipment (that he had bought) in the center of the campground - an Ampeg SVT, Marshall stacks, Twin Reverbs, a complete drum kit and sound system. He poured gasoline on it and lit it afire. It was his statement to show us just who was in charge. He stood there and glared at us, arms akimbo and defiant. I looked at Stiv and he at me. We bolted over to our Winnebago. I grabbed a couple of sticks and some lawn chairs and Stiv pulled a pack of hot dogs from the refrigerator. We went back to the fire and proceeded to have a wiener roast. Eddy Best took a photo of Stiv and I roasting wienies. This was the LAST STRAW! Our former benefactor was now racing toward us holding an aluminum ladder over his head, eyes bulging and swearing in French. He hit Stiv with the ladder. The Great Campaign Tour Of 1979 was in shambles.

The Retreat From Ridgecrest

We knew we had to get out of Ridgecrest. We walked into town, found a pay phone and called our friend Greg Shaw in LA. 'Greg, please send the cavalry'. The Real Kids (who had been unlucky enough to be in Greg's office when the call came) volunteered to rescue us. When they arrived 3 hours later blowing the horn and circling the wagons, we greeted them like long lost brothers. Now safely on our way, we stopped to pick up some take-out sandwiches. Barely out of Ridgecrest, turning a corner the van sped out of control and off the road throwing Stiv and I from the back to the front. I was alright but Stiv wasn't moving. We thought he was faking at first... then he started turning blue. He was choking. I started to give him the Heimlich maneuver, but it wasn't working. I kept trying harder and harder. Finally he popped out a piece of sausage that had been lodged in the back of his throat. He started coming around and asked what happened? I said, 'You owe me ten bucks. I saved your life'. He laughed and gave me the ten and said thanks, 'Cause if he had died you know what the papers would have said – "Caught With The Meat In HIS Mouth".

Disconnected And Putting It All In Perspective

In April of 1979, we formally hooked up with Greg Shaw and Bomp Records. We all had the same musical tastes, had the same vision and were the same age. It was a good combination. Stiv wanted to do something really different after the Dead Boys.

Our first 45rpm on which we were joined by Eddy Best (guitar) and Rick Bremmer (drums) was *It's Cold Outside* b/w *The Last Year* and was released in May, '79. It was well received. We followed it with *Not That Way Anymore* b/w *Circumstantial Evidence* between Dead Boys tours. Speaking of which, starting in October 1979 when the original group was set to go on tour again, Jeff Magnum bailed at the last moment and I was called to replace him. After one day's rehearsal, I flew with the group to Toronto (incidentally our part in the "DOA" movie was filmed that night).

That line-up: Stiv, Jimmy, Cheetah, Johnny and I would last until December when Cheetah broke his wrist at Keith Richard's birthday party at the Roxy Roller Disco in New York. With a national tour set to begin in a few days and Cheetah incapacitated, we asked ace guitarist George Cabaniss of Akron's Hammer Damage Band if he would join us. That line-up: Stiv, Frank, George, Jimmy and Johnny crisscrossed North America for the next 6 months. All the while the group promoted Stiv's Bomp singles and decidedly started taking on a more pop direction to the sometimes utter dismay of the hard core folks who were showing up at the gigs, but the band always put on a good show. Striped coats and Beatle boots started to appear, and Johnny left the band in May, 1980. Nineteen year old wiz-kid drummer David Quinton Steinberg from Toronto's 'Mods' (who had already played on the *Not That Way Anymore* single in the summer of 1979) joined us in L.A. for the Whisky A Go-Go job in late May.

One last tour in the summer of '80 saw Jimmy Zero leaving, and with a recording date set in August at Perspective Studios in Sun Valley, California, the line-up for the 'Disconnected' LP would be Stiv (lead vocals, guitar) George Cabaniss (lead guitar), David Quinton Steinberg (drums, piano) and myself on bass guitar. In addition to being top-notch musicians, Cabaniss and Quinton (we were soon to find) were first-rate songwriters contributing *Swinging A Go-Go, Make Up Your Mind,* and *Bad Luck Charm* between them.

Now, for Stiv and I, the endless days at the Sunset Marquis and in the desert had paid off for 'Disconnected' in the form of some very creative songs which were written there., *A Million Miles Away, I'll Be Alright, Circumstantial Evidence, Ready Anytime, Not That Way Anymore* and *I Wanna Forget You (Just The Way You Are)* were all written there. We also had *Evil Boy* that Jimmy Zero and I had written that summer in Cleveland. I'm not going to talk about the music of 'Disconnected', as I've always felt that music does or doesn't speak for itself. I will however talk about the fun we had making it. It's true - 'Disconnected was recorded on a basketball court that was adjacent to the studio. The wooden floor had an extremely "live" sound, so we did most of the basic tracks there. Cynthia Ross and the fabulous B-Girls from Canada came to town and added harmonies and hand-claps for *Swinging A Go-Go*. For the explosion sound on *Too Much To Dream*, Stiv and I dropped a Fender Twin Reverb amp (rented of course) off a ladder and recorded it (hey, go ahead try that at home kids). While recording *Ready Anytime* Stiv couldn't quite get the vocal the way he wanted. He said he had to go to Hollywood to get some inspiration. We did overdubs while he was gone until he returned 4 hours later very drunk with some girl. He went in the vocal booth and started to perform while out of our sight she performed on him. It was a keeper. To top it all off for the real climax of the album, I wanted an 1812 Overture type ending for *I Wanna Forget You (Just The Way You Are)* - big, bombastic and over the top. An audio Napoleonic Wars cannonade it was to be! We got our friend Kent Smythe to bring in thousands of fireworks. We dutifully and strategically placed microphones around the fireworks we had fused together and producer Thom Wilson started rolling the tape as Stiv and I lit them on fire. ONE MAJOR PROBLEM! As the fire works went off the studio immediately filled with smoke. In the midst of all the explosions, Stiv and I couldn't see or breathe. We were suffocating and choking and had to literally crawl for our lives out of the studio while David, George, Thom and Kent were falling about laughing. We spent the rest of the session clearing the smoke out of the studio. To top it off, when we played it back it sounded so fucking crazy we couldn't use it. Here, without you here, without you here...

That night on the drive back to Hollywood from the studio, Stiv and David were driving in the car ahead of me with a couple of girls at 75mph down the freeway. Stiv crawled out the window, stood on the roof and proceeded to engage in a 'sick' sport (that he alone invented) called "car surfing". I had seen this many times back home, but on the LA freeway with thousands of cars at night, it made me particularly nervous. Stiv sensing this, looked back at me and smiled. Then, he dropped his pants to his ankles. He wasn't wearing any underwear. I almost wrecked the car laughing.

I miss you Stiv.

Frank Secich - June 6, 2004

DISCONNECTED OFFSPRING AND DELUSIONS OF GRANDEUR

George Cabaniss

George teamed up with Marti Jones in 1982 and formed 'Color Me Gone' in Akron. They were signed to A&M Records and released a fabulous EP containing the single he wrote called *Lose Control*, a stunning record which I personally consider the best 45rpm of the 1980's. Marti went solo and Color Me Gone was gone. It's a high crime that this is not available on CD. George lives and works in the Youngstown-Akron area.

David 'Quinton' Steinberg

In 1981, David recorded a solo album for Bomb Records in Canada. The self-titled 'David Quinton' is a power pop marvel that has been re-released on CD by Bullseye Records as 'Bombs and Lullabies'. His old band from the late 1970's, The Mods have also been reissued on CD by Other People's Music. Today, David is an entertainment attorney in Toronto.

Thom Wilson

Greg and I think 'Disconnected' may have been the first record Thom Wilson ever produced. It won the NAIRD award for the Best Independent Album of 1981. Today, Thom Wilson is a world-famous producer of Offspring, Iggy Pop. New Edition, Madonna, Dead Kennedys, TSOL, Karma and others.

Greg Shaw

Bomp Records still going after 30 years. Greg is a record man and a visionary. He's a shaker and a mover in the grand tradition of Jerry Wexler, Herb Abramson, Phil Spector and Sam Phillips. I can give him no higher compliment.

Frank Secich

Joined 'Club Wow' in Cleveland with Jimmy Zero, Billy Sullivan and Jeff West from 1982-85, then produced 'The Infidels' and others over the next 5 years. In 1990, went on a self-imposed exile to the remote island of St. Helena in the South Atlantic for inspiration. He returned in 2003 and reformed his old group 'Blue Ash' with all original members and they are released a 2CD retrospective called 'Around Again' on Not Lame in the summer of 2004. In 2007 along with Terry Hartman, Pete Drivere and John Koury formed the Deadbeat Poets who working on their 8th album in 2015.

Stiv Bators

When we finished 'Disconnected', Stiv went to Baltimore to film "Polyester" with John Waters, then to England to record with 'The Wanderers'. The 'Disconnected' album was released the week John Lennon was killed in New York. We did a small tour in the Northeast with Brian James that December and January to support the album. In January, Stiv relocated to England joined 'The Wanderers' and the following year started the 'Lords of the New Church'. In May 1990, Stiv was recording a new solo album in France. One of the songs he cut was a pretty ballad written by Jimmy Zero and Frank Secich called *You Don't Go Away*. Two weeks later, he was hit by a car in Paris and died the following day from internal injuries.

Recording Circumstantial Evidence

While we were recording 'Circumstantial Evidence', I didn't like the 3rd verse so I changed it before Stiv did the vocals. I handed it to him. 'Just fill in the blanks with couple of girls names'.

My girlfriend.____ heard about me all alone
With her best friend_____ , over the telephone
She said you look me in the eye and
Tell me it was just a lie
She's giving the third degree
She's convinced that I'm a guilty and
She wants me guillotined

He looked over in the corner at my wife and Joan Jett talking and said Joan and Lisa.

CIRCUMSTANTIAL EVIDENCE

(Secich-Bators)

The Detective Lieutenant called me to the police station
While pursuing the investigation He said "Where were you last night at ten
When the corner store was broken into?"
You were seen roaming the neighborhood and
We know that you did it
We know it was you

Circumstantial evidence is all you got on me
Circumstantial evidence you can't pin a thing on me

The Principal called me to the office room
About a run-in with a teacher,I had in my home room
It goes in one ear and out the other
Don't know why I should bother
I'm telling you with that attitude
You won't last very long around here
Do I make myself clear

Circumstantial evidence is all you got on me
Circumstantial evidence you can't pin a thing on me

It really makes me laugh
When I look at your photographs
How you rained so ugly on my parade
When I think about it looking back

My girlfriend. Joan heard about me all alone
With her best friend Lisa, over the telephone
She said you look me in the eye and
Tell me it was just a lie
She's giving the third degree
She's convinced that I'm a guilty and
She wants me guillotined

Circumstantial evidence is all you got on me
Circumstantial evidence you can't pin a thing on me
Can't pin a thing on me
Can't pin a thing on me

The Gutter Twins

Stiv and I had written *The Last Year* in October of 1978 at my apartment on the West Hill in Sharon, Pennsylvania. In November of that year we made a demo tape at Kirk Yano's 'After Dark Studio' in Cleveland. Playing on the demo were Jimmy Zero (guitar), Johnny Blitz (drums), Stiv (vocals, tambourine) and me on bass guitar. The songs we recorded were *It's Cold Outside* and *The Last Year*. Stiv and his then girlfriend Cynthia Ross from the B-Girls went to Los Angeles to do some promotion for the great B-Girls single *Fun At The Beach* which had been released on Bomp Records. Stiv played the demo for Greg Shaw and he was quite taken by it. After our adventures in the desert, we (Eddy Best, Rick Bremmer, Stiv and myself) had taken up residency at the Tropicana motel in West Hollywood. Greg came over and asked us if we'd like to record for Bomp Records. We loved the Bomp set-up and artistic freedom we knew Greg would give us. Soon after, we went into 'Bijou Studios' in Hollywood with Greg and the "Gutter Twins" (Stiv and I) producing. Greg also hired a British engineer named David Zammit. The first song we tackled was the Choir's classic *It's Cold Outside*. We sped the song up considerably and wanted a 'wall of power' so we put seven guitars on it. Stiv played the Vox Phantom, I played a Mosrite bass, a Fender Stratocaster, my Rickenbacker and the Phantom while Eddy Best played a Rickenbacker 12-string, the Rick 6-string and bass-heavy Stratocaster. Stiv then added his lead vocal and Stiv and I did the background vocals and handclaps (which was Greg's idea) during the power-chorded solo. When we played it back we knew we were on to something different. We approached *The Last Year* in similar fashion. Stiv and Eddy playing the rhythm guitars and Eddy and I played the lead in harmony and I added the 12-string parts. The vocals are Stiv and I singing two part harmony through the entire song. We finished the entire project, mix and everything that same night. The next day we put it to the true test as we drove around LA in Greg's Trans-Am and blasted it through the speakers. It passed. It was definitely a cruisin' song.

When Stiv and I got the acetates of *It's Cold Outside* we went over to Rodney Bingenheimer's apartment and played it for him. Rodney invited us to be his guests on his next KROQ show. On the air the first thing Rodney asked after introducing us was 'So what have you guys been up to?' Stiv jokingly said 'We've been very busy running around the hills starting all those forest fires' and I chimed in...'but we had to stop 'cause we ran out of matches'. I think Rodney always liked having us on his show. That summer (1979) we had a lot of fun promoting that record. The record started breaking out in New York City. It was getting tons of airplay on WNEW and WPIX and selling well in the city. Greg decided to send Stiv and I there on a promotional tour accompanied by Merle Hauser who worked for Bomp. Stiv came to the city with his then girlfriend, super-model Bebe Buell. Bebe was a smart girl and had a great personality and funny sense of humor. She and Stiv used to sing a duet of the old song *Hey Paula*. I wish I had that on tape. It was very funny and good. While we were doing the interview in WPIX on the air, Stiv invited all of New York to come down the Mudd Club that evening for Bebe's birthday party. There were a lot of people when we arrived there. Later that night at the Mudd Club we jammed with Johnny Thunders, Rick Derringer and David Johansen. I have to say - it was always interesting, as you'd never know who would show up on any given night.

Hollywood Swinging

'LA Confidential' wouldn't live up to its name if I couldn't tell the glamorous part of the seedy story. Stiv and I were huge fans of Paul Revere and the Raiders. One of our finest moments happened at a record release party that Kim Fowley threw for his newest discovery, an all-girl group called the Orchids. Kim gathered Stiv and I and said, 'Stiv and Frank there's someone I'd like you to meet. Guys, this is 'Fang'. We had met a lot of famous people but we were 'AWESTRUCK' meeting our hero, Phil Volk of the Raiders. Later on at the party I nudged Stiv and said 'Can you believe we're out here making cool records, with all these crazy parties and hangin' out with the Raiders - and they're paying us for it? How cool is that?' Stiv said, 'I know'.

Then there was the time we met actor Dick Van Dyke in the parking lot of a dry cleaners on Sunset Blvd. and while he signed an autograph for us, I'm supposed to keep a straight face as Stiv said to him 'Mr. Van Dyke this is a great honor, especially for me. You see, I grew up in an orphanage in Ohio and the only TV they let us watch once a week was the 'Dick Van Dyke Show'. Then Stiv became almost tearful and with a pathetic voice looked Van Dyke in the eye and said, 'You were like the dad, I never had'. Stiv went on and on with him, 'In fact you've inspired me to do what I do today'. Van Dyke takes the bait...'What's that?' 'I'm a singer in a punk band'. 'Well, guys nice talking to you... I've gotta run'. After Dick drove off I asked Stiv, 'Where did you come up with that?' Stiv just laughed.

Long Live The Chields

One time in the late 1960's, I booked a gig at an outdoor show on the outskirts of Youngstown, Ohio. There were many local bands on the bill. The only problem was that I was between bands and didn't have a group. I told the promoter it was a mystery group. I gathered some musicians, Myron Grombacher (drums) who would later become famous as Pat Benetar's drummer, Steve Acker (guitar), Bill 'Goog' Yendrek (guitar), me on bass and a crazy friend of mine named Steve would be the singer and harmonica player - only Steve didn't have a harmonica. He would cup his hands and make harmonica sounds with his mouth. You could not tell the difference. It was remarkable. This would be Mr. Bators first time on stage. We had to have a name, so I (jokingly) asked Goog's sister Anna to name the group. She said call it The Chields. I said 'What the hell does that mean?' She just giggled. I looked it up. Chield is the plural for the Scottish word: 'chiel' which means young man. So chields must be a double, multiple plural of it. So 'The Chields' it was.

We started off the show with *Stray Cat Blues* and we kept building momentum as we were flying across the stage and generally having a great time. Starting our last song *Kick Out The Jams*, I noticed that Steve pulled out a can of whipped cream. He started shaking the can in his crotch area, then let the cream shoot into the crowd. The audience went crazy. He had them now. Next, he threw the microphone stand straight up in the air. I didn't notice at the time, but it had clipped his head on the way down. He had a gash in his head and was bleeding. Then he started smearing the whipped cream on himself and it was mixing with the blood. As I looked over, he had this orangish-colored cream covering him. The audience thought it was an act, but none of it was rehearsed. He was truly hurt. He kept on and got a great ovation. I took him right away to the emergency room to get stitched up. His reputation spread, and he was asked to join the infamous 'Mother Goose Band' and now you know the start of the story.

The Great Photographers

As Marianne Faithfull once told me 'I've always thought that the artwork was just as important as the music'. I have had the honor and privilege of working with some of the best Rock & Roll photographers in the world. These are the folks who have always made us look good through their vision and their talents. Donna Santisi took that great photo for the Stiv Bators' *It's Cold Outside* picture sleeve. Goldmine Magazine named that sleeve as one of the best picture sleeves ever. Donna's photo of us with John Belushi at the Whisky A Go-Go was also featured in People Magazine in 1980. She has sent me some ultra rare photos of me, Stiv and the band which will appear in this book for the first time anywhere.

David Arnoff took the great photo on the front of Stiv's 'Disconnected' LP 1980. David has a cool new book coming out called Shot In The Dark.

Theresa Kereakes took the cool back cover shots on 'Disconnected' as well as the inner sleeve. Theresa has also kindly let us use her great photography throughout this book. She also took the back cover of this book.

Mick Rock is also one of the greats. Stiv and I were at a party in New York once and Mick was there. We told him we need a great photo for our new single *Not That Way Anymore*, so he said, 'Okay, I'll be right back'. We didn't mean right then at the party. Mick returns with a ladder and a camera and gets on the ladder and says 'Look up'. He was very loaded and teetering on the ladder as he took four photos. He then said 'I've got it', Stiv said 'We usually take hundreds of photos then pick'. Mick just laughed and said 'No need... Wait until you see this last one'. I have the four negatives: one shot is out of focus, one shot twisted up, the other was not a good photo but the fourth is the iconic one you see on the *Not That Way Anymore* Bomp Records picture sleeve.

David Gahr (who took so many classic photos of Bob Dylan, Sonny Terry, Janis Joplin, John Lennon, Bruce Springsteen, Miles Davis, Johnny Cash and so many others) was hired by Paul Nelson of Mercury to take the Blue Ash LP photos and Mercury publicity photos. David passed away in 2008. What an honor it was to have him photograph us.

Bob Gruen took the pic of me, Jim Kendzor and Yoko that appeared in all the rock magazines is another legendary photographer. You'll also see many photos in the book by Geoff Jones who was also a talented man with a camera. I'd also like to give a special shout out to my old friend Frank Laudo who has done such a fantastic job with the artwork on all of the Deadbeat Poets projects.

60

TERRY HARTMAN – THE MAN WITH THE X-RAY EYES

The Man With The X-Ray Eyes b/w *Down With The Lonely Boys* by Terry and the Tornados.

In 1980, Jimmy Zero from the Dead Boys and I had arranged with Greg Shaw to put out a single on Bomp by Terry and the Tornadoes. Jimmy would produce it at Kirk Yano's After Dark Studio in Cleveland. Jimmy asked me to play on the single. Terry Hartman at that time was America's great unknown songwriter. Jimmy, Greg and I were going to change that. They had already recorded Terry's classic *Down With The Lonely Boys* and brought me in to play bass and guitar on *The Man With The X-Ray Eyes*. They also brought Johnny Blitz in to drum. Johnny turned in one of his finest and most powerful performances. I also added an organ part and Kevin Kierer played acoustic guitar. My pay was a fifth of Tangueray Gin. Greg loved the single and was ready to run with it but it was never released. At the time he was having company problems and wasn't releasing anything on Bomp for a while and had to put everything off. It's a wonderful recording.

In the last 6 months before Greg died in 2004, I was constantly in touch with him doing the massive liner notes. Greg told me one of his biggest regrets was not getting to release the Terry and the Tornados single. I eventually made it good to Terry when I asked him to join the Deadbeat Poets. The Deadbeat Poets recording of *The Man With The X-Ray Eyes* was picked by Little Steven as 'Coolest Song In The World' in 2011 and voted by the worldwide fans of the show as #5 'Coolest Song In The World For The Year 2011'. It's found on our Pop Detective CD 'Youngstown Vortex Sutra (The British Version)'. *Down With The Lonely Boys* was also rerecorded by the Deadbeat Poets and is on the 'American Stroboscope' album of 2012. Finally as a Deadbeat Poet, after all these years the world has been introduced to Terry's talent and will continue to be entertained by his genius.

61

STIV BATORS BAND – THE DEAD BOYS TOURS AND THE ADVENTURES OF 1979-81

MARIANNE FAITHFULL, ANITA PALLENBURG AND NICO – 1979

As I mentioned earlier in the summer of 1979, Greg Shaw sent Stiv and I on a promo tour to New York City along with Bomp Records' VP Merle Hauser to promote our new 45, *It's Cold Outside*. As we ended our interview at WPIX, I looked through the studio glass to see no other than Marianne Faithfull and Merle Hauser talking and Merle was showing her the picture sleeve of *It's Cold Outside*. I couldn't believe it. There was Marianne Faithfull and she was as drop dead gorgeous as Marianne Faithfull should be. She was there to do an interview after us. As I walked out of the booth she walked up to me holding the picture sleeve and said with her charming British accent 'What a great picture sleeve, I've always thought that the artwork is just as important as the music'. Then she held out her hand to me and said 'I'm sorry, I'm Marianne'.

It was July 14, 1979 and it was Bebe Buell's birthday. Stiv had been going out with Bebe for a while and we were having a party at the Mudd Club that night for her. I asked Marianne and her friends if they'd like to come and they did. While we were on the air. Stiv invited everyone in NY to come down to the Mudd Club and celebrate Bebe's birthday. When we got to the club there were a lot of people outside. As we were standing there I felt a tap on my shoulder. I turned around and it was John McEnroe with Vitus Gerulaitis and two beautiful girls. John said 'Mind if we crash your party? We heard you on the radio and it sounded like fun'. Anita Pallenberg and Nico also showed up as they did to quite a few of our gigs. Debbie Harry was there as well. So, we partied with all of them that night. Stiv and I later got up and jammed with David Johansen, Johnny Thunders, Rick Derringer and Clem Burke. I remember we did *Pills, Trash* and a few other songs and it sounded very good.

LET THE MIDNIGHT SPECIAL SHINE ITS EVER LOVING LIGHT

In early 1979, both Stiv and I had discovered The Records from England and had bought their indie import single *Starry Eyes* and became big fans. We were in New York City later in June and July to promote *It's Cold Outside*, doing radio shows and promotions. Stiv went to see a friend at Virgin Records and while visiting there his friend played him the new album soon to be released by The Records and the bonus EP that came with it. The EP starts with a cover of Blue Ash's *Abracadabra (Have You Seen Her?)*. There is no greater honor or compliment for a songwriter than to have a song covered and especially covered by a world-class group like The Records. Their album and single stormed up the charts in the power pop summer of 1979.

Stiv and I went back to LA to record in August and September of 1979. Lisa was also out there with me. We all went to see and meet The Records on the Midnight Special at NBC in Burbank where the Cars and Iggy Pop were also on the show. We had a great time meeting and talking to Will Birch, John Wicks, Phil Brown and Huw Gower. I'm still in touch with Will Birch and John Wicks and they are two of the finest and most talented gentlemen I've known in this business.

DOA MOVIE - ORIENTAL ROCK PLACE TORONTO, ONTARIO - OCTOBER 1979

I got a call on the night of October 23 from Stiv and he asked me if I could play some dates with the Dead Boys in Canada on the 25, 26 and 27th of October. He says, 'You have the albums just learn the songs and we'll fly you up to NY on the 24th and rehearse all day and fly to Toronto the next day'. That's what I did. They were also filming the movie 'DOA (A Rite Of Passage)' at the shows these three days. These would be my first dates with The Dead Boys. I sat next to Cheetah on the flight to Toronto. As we were on our way I asked him if he had manifests and working papers for Canada as I knew from Blue Ash playing there a few years before you always needed such things. Cheetah says 'No, I don't have any of that'. So, were going through customs and a young customs agent says 'Hey, Cheetah Chrome, The Dead Boys, I'll take care of you guys' and he let us right through which was cool. He then asked Cheetah to put him on the guest list that night.

The three days at the Oriental Rock Palace was a wild affair. On the third and last night a major fight broke out all through the audience and the Toronto Police were called in to clear the place. I remember one guy was really beat up and his teeth were smashed in and they're pushing him about and he's yelling at the cops until they finally believed him 'I'm an off duty policeman you assholes, I was just here enjoying the concert'.

I was glad to be playing with the band as I always thought they sounded amazing live. Cheetah and Jimmy's guitar interaction was mesmerizing. I always enjoyed Magnum's playing as well even though I was now filling in for him. Blitz was the one who pushed it all over the top. I was going to have a fun next one and a half years.

MEETING THE ROLLING STONES - DECEMBER 18 1979

One of the funniest things I ever saw Stiv do happened the night we met the Rolling Stones on December 18, 1979. We were invited by Anita Pallenberg to Keith Richard's 36th birthday party in New York City. It was a private party at the Roxy Roller Disco. Our guitarist Cheetah Chrome was there first and fell and broke his wrist while roller skating before we got there. Stiv, Jimmy Zero and I arrived a little later. As soon as we got there Anita introduced us to Keith and Ron Wood which was great. The first thing Keith said to us was 'Your Cheetah really did it, he fell and broke is wrist. My driver took him to the hospital'. Keith was everything you think he'd be. He's one of the coolest guys in the world. Mick Jagger was at the party too but we didn't get to meet him at first. Later on in the evening we saw Mick standing in the middle of the room talking to Bobby Keyes and a Jamaican guy. Stiv started walking toward them. I looked at Zero and said we'd better go with him because he's going to do something.

Stiv walks up to Mick from behind and taps him on the shoulder. Slowly, Mick turns around with the most condescending look I've ever seen. Mick was on roller skates which made him seem very tall and he holding a bottle of Michelob beer... I'm not kidding. Then Bators says 'Where's the men's room?" Jagger goes.... What????? Then Stiv loudly says 'I SAID, where's the men's room?' Mick shakes his head and points 'It's over there around the corner'. The three of us then went to the rest room and once inside fell about the room, almost pissing ourselves and laughing. I told Stiv 'I can't believe you did that'. Mick was his hero and he just had to do something like that. That was how Stiv was. The Stones were always our idols and that was a great night and memory.

WHISKY A GO-GO JANUARY 26TH, 27TH, 28TH - 1980

The Dead Boys were booked at the famed Whisky A Go-Go in LA for three consecutive nights the 26, 27 and 28th of January in 1980. We did two shows a night and sold out all of them. On the first night, Friday the 26th we had a very special guest come up and play drums with us and that was the legendary actor and comedian, John Belushi. John was a huge fan of the band but it was the first time I'd met him. After we finished our set we got a rousing encore. When we came back to the stage Stiv got on the microphone and said 'There's this guy back stage who has been bugging us to let him come up and play the drums on *Sonic Reducer* So we're going to bring him out'. As John climbed on the drum riser the applause built into a deafening roar as the crowd realized who it was. John was one of the biggest stars in the world then as this was right after Animal House and The Blues Brothers. We did a blistering rendition of *Sonic Reducer* and the jam packed crowd went manic and wild. As we finished the song the roar sounded like the Beatles at Shea Stadium even though the club probably had only 600 jammed inside. I never heard anything like it. After we finished the song in the midst of all this mayhem John jumped off the drum riser and walked right up to me. He shook my hand then he yelled in my ear 'Did I fuck up?' And I said 'No, you were great!' Then he bowed to the crowd. Afterward we went back up to the upstairs dressing room and partied for about an hour. Then John went next door to the Roxy and jammed with Muddy Waters. The next night Joan Jett joined us on stage. The next week there was a feature story about us and John and Joan along with photos that Donna Santisi took of that wild night in People Magazine. It was a night I'll never forget.

62

JOHNNY BLITZ AND HIS FABULOUS DEAD BOYS

There's probably never been a rock group of more colorful characters ever than The Dead Boys. When I played with them 1979-81 it was like being in a comedy movie and a horror movie at the same time. Never a dull moment. I will describe some of the adventures in the following series of Dead Boy vignettes.

ANN ARBOR THE SECOND CHANCE

The first gig of the Dead Boys February-March of 1980 winter tour was a place called the Second Chance in Ann Arbor, Michigan. The Testors, a great band featuring Sonny Vincent and Jeff West would be the opening band for the tour and we would be using their back line. Ann Arbor is the home of the University of Michigan. The Michigan-Ohio State rivalry is one of the most legendary in American sports. The Second Chance was packed that night with about 600 people. It was the first night of our national tour. There was also a balcony that came down close to the stage. We came out and we're burning through our set sounding pretty good and the crowd was really into the show. About 45 minutes into the show it started getting a little wild.

Then someone threw a beer mug from the balcony that hit Johnny Blitz in the leg. Blitz jumped from behind the drums, grabbed the microphone from Stiv and challenged the person who had thrown the mug, to come down from the balcony and fight him like a man. Then Blitz said 'You know I've played all over the world and nothing like this ever happened, I come to Ann Arbor and get hit with a beer mug'. Then Blitz offered $500 to whoever threw it to come down and fight him. We were laughing our asses off on stage. No one would accept Johnny's challenge... He began to walk back to the drums (wearing his Ohio State football jersey)... has second thoughts then turns and goes back to the microphone. 'One more thing, your football team SUCKS!' All hell broke loose. The audience began to rain glass mugs down on us. Our fans then started fighting with the rowdies. A riot ensued. There was glass breaking and flying everywhere and we bolted off the stage as fast as we could. Our road manager, Geoff Jones went back to get our back up guitars that were still on stage using a table as a shield. The police arrived and broke up the fight and made everyone evacuate the premises. The next day the headline on the front page of the Ann Arbor newspaper (with a photo of us and all the damage) read: 'DEAD BOYS AND FANS ENGAGE IN SECOND CHANCE MELEE'. When we passed through Ann Arbor three weeks later places were selling buttons that read 'I survived The Dead Boys in the Second Chance'. I bought one.

STIV! STIV!...... BANDIT AT ONE O'CLOCK

I'll give Stiv his due as a world-class prankster, piss-taker and inventor and master of 'Car Surfing' and 'Drink and Release' (don't ask).... but 'Puddle Splashing' was my invention (driving close enough to a curb where water has accumulated then speeding up and soaking pedestrians on the sidewalk). I also invented leaning out the window of a moving car and tapping someone with a broom called 'Brooming' which comically appeared in the John Waters' movie 'Polyester' without the slightest credit to it's creator. Anyway, we were playing in Toronto and had just done a sound check in the afternoon and returned to the Delta Chelsea Inn. Geoff Jones tossed the keys to the car to Stiv and handed me a note with an address and said 'You two have to do an in-store at this record store on Queen St. at 5:00pm', so we took off. After we finished the in-store promotion Stiv and I went down Queen and turned north on Yonge toward the Chelsea Inn and at about a block before Dundas I yelled 'Stiv! Stiv!..... Bandit at one o'clock!' Stiv excitedly 'I see it! I see it!' There about a half of a block before us on the right was a nice looking woman probably in her late 30's or early 40's , dressed to the hilt. She's was wearing a mink or sable coat which was fashionable with rich women in Toronto at the time. She was smiling. She was probably waiting there for her lover and a dinner at a fancy restaurant and then maybe a romantic evening at the Pantages. She was what she probably thought was a fair distance from the street and never even noticed a three foot wide slush puddle that had formed out from the curb in front of her. Little did she know she was in the cross hairs of two master Puddle Splashers. 'Stiv, you only have one shot, 35 mph and hit the puddle at 18 inches from the curb'. 'I know, I know! Green light! Perfect! SPPPPLLLLLAAAAASSSSHHHHH! As the slush cascaded over her from head to foot. I looked back and she was soaking wet and frozen in shock. We never laughed so hard in our lives.

THE HOT CLUB, PHILLY, DAVE, DRUGS AND READING IGGY'S MIND

One time while we were playing a bunch of gigs in the New York, New Jersey and Long Island area we had a rare day off. Stiv, Cheetah, Jimmy and I hired a limousine and went to see Iggy at the Hot Club in Philadelphia on South St. which was run by a great guy nicknamed Dave Drugs. The Hot Club was one of the wildest places I've ever played and I mean that in a good way. The floor sloped down toward the stage and the place was always packed and there was no room left or right for the band to exit the stage. The audience would lift people in the air and pass them downward to the stage then throw them toward the stage and there would be spit everywhere. It was wild and I always loved playing there for some reason. We had played there a few times before. It was the quintessential punk experience to either play or attend as an audience member. So, we off went to see Iggy. He was great and put on a wild show as always. Afterward we were backstage with the band and having a great time. We were talking with Iggy and having a great time until he got a funny look on his face and just kind of went in the corner. He started talking to his road manager and the road manger said us 'Jim (they always call him by his real name) Jim, says you have to leave and you have to leave right now'. And one of us said 'What's up? What's wrong?' Jim says 'You're reading his mind and stealing his ideas'. We just howled.

BOB SEGARINI, LARRY'S HIDEAWAY, TORONTO

When Stiv and Cynthia Ross were visiting Lisa and I at our apartment in Sharon at Christmas time, 1978. Cynthia asked me 'Do you know Bob Segarini?' I said, 'No, but I'd like to meet him some day because I've been a fan of his since 1968 and the Miss Butters album by Family Tree'. Cyn, said 'You'd get along great with him cause you guys are like the same person'. So, the Dead Boys rolled into the famed Larry's Hideaway in March of 1980. We didn't have roadies with us so we hired some local Canadian roadies which was a big mistake. My 1966, Rickenbacker guitar which we used as a back up on stage was stolen from the stage while the roadies were supposedly watching our gear. I'm sure today that they were in on it. Anyway it was a pretty good show and we had a dressing room on the third floor of the hotel I finally got to meet Bob Segarini there and we talked for a good while in the hallway outside the dressing room. Suddenly we heard a loud crash and a window breaking. Bob without missing a beat says to me 'There goes your pay tonight'. Out come Blitz and Bators laughing like crazy. They had not only thrown the TV out of the window of the hotel they threw it right through the French window as it fell 3 stories to the ground. In storms Geoff Jones very pissed. 'The owner was actually handing me your money and as he heard the noise he just pulled it back. He took enough out of your pay to pay for the window and TV'.

To add insult to injury, when you played in Canada as an American back then you had to put a deposit on your guitar so you wouldn't sell it in Canada and when you left Canada you got you're $300.00 deposit back when you showed them the guitar as you were leaving. I got a Toronto police report about my stolen guitar and turned it in at customs but they wouldn't give me my deposit back.

CALL THE FLY ATTENDANT

There was a novelty store on North Water Ave. in Sharon and we'd always load up with rubber flies and cockroaches and exploding cigarettes fuses and things like that before a tour. When we were flying somewhere as soon as we were seated we'd tie the barf bags under our chins. Once the meals were served we'd go into comedy mode. Stiv would put a rubber fly or cockroach in his food. He'd then pick it up with a fork and show all the passengers who could see and hear him. 'Look at this, this was in my meal', to moans of passengers like 'Oh that's disgusting', 'my God' etc.... Then Stiv would call over the stewardess. 'Miss!!! Miss!!!! Excuse me, Miss, look what was in my food' She'd say 'Oh that's disgusting' and Stiv would say 'I think it's either a cockroach or a fly' then he'd pick it up with his fingers and shove it in his mouth and start chewing as everyone around grimaced then he'd say 'It's a fly!' Call the fly attendant' as I would snap a photo of the horrified stewardesses and passengers. We had dozens of photos of flight attendants like that.

One time after we did it and we all had a good laugh, one of the flight attendants comes over to me and asks if she can borrow my fly. I skeptically inquired 'What for?'. 'We're going to play a little trick on the Captain'. I said 'I don't know'. She said 'He's a great guy and has a great sense of humor... don't worry'. I said 'I don't like the idea of screwing with guy's meal who's responsible for hundreds of lives and millions of dollars worth of equipment'. She said 'It'll be alright', I said 'Okay, but I lend you this cockroach under protest'. About 15 minutes later she was walking down the aisle with her head down. I asked 'What happened?' She whispered 'He just threw the tray aside'. 'You didn't tell him you did it, did you?' She said 'No way', I said, 'You owe me a cockroach'.

GRAMERCY PARK HOTEL AND SUSAN SARANDON

A lot of rock stars used to stay at the Gramercy Park Hotel. It was a classic old New York hotel with a big revolving door at the entrance. Stiv and I were at the desk checking in and I saw Jimmy Zero walk over to the revolving door. There was a guy entering the door from the street side. It was a well-known diminutive English pop star but I don't want to embarrass him. As he's almost in the hotel, Zero puts his foot out and blocks the revolving door trapping him inside. He keeps trying to force the door but to no avail. He's getting panicky and Jimmy is yelling at him. 'It's stuck! It's stuck!' While still holding his foot there. Bators and I are in tears. Jimmy finally let him in.

The same time while we were staying in the Gramercy Park hotel in New York City and the phone rang and it was our friend Kirk Wood from LA. Kirk was an entertainment attorney and was friends with Susan Sarandon. I had answered the phone and Kirk told me 'Susan's in town and she'd like to meet you guys. Is it alright if she comes over in about half an hour?' I said 'Sure'. Stiv said who called? I said it was Kirk and he said Susan Sarandon was on her way over and Stiv goes 'Really'. Geoff Jones says 'I'll go out and get some food and wine'. So, half an hour later there's a knock on our door which I opened 'Hi. I'm Susan... Did Kirk call you guys?' Susan was very cool and partied and hung out with us (Stiv, Bebe Buell, Jimmy Zero, Geoff Jones and me) all evening. Susan and Bebe both are two of the great ladies of all time. Geoff took some great photos of the night as well. Stiv and I were going to be in a movie around that time that Kirk was going to produce. Jimmy and I even wrote a few songs for it, my *Sweet Little F-16* and Jimmy's *Life In The War Zone* but the movie never got made. You will however get a chance to see the video Club Wow made of *Life In The War Zone* on the upcoming Club Wow CD/DVD set on Zero Hour Records.

THE DEAD BOYS - DETROIT TO BOSTON IN A PROP PLANE

Geoff Jones always had his hands full with us but on this day Stiv showed up very late in the morning back to our hotel after carousing all night and we missed our flight to Boston where we had to play that night. Geoff, resourceful as always found a small airline in Detroit that had an old prop plane that was going to Boston. We sped to the airport and caught the flight just in time. Geoff would drive and meet us in Hartford, Connecticut in 3 days but we'd be our own in Boston and Willamantic, Connecticut. Certain members of the band did not like flying at all and had to be very drunk to even get on a plane. Johnny who was one of the toughest men I'd ever met and a street fighter who wouldn't back down from a fight with anyone but was terrified of flying as half of the population of America is. So, as we walked on the tarmac to the steps leading into the prop plane, Johnny turns to Geoff and says 'Jonesey, What have you done? You've killed the Dead Boys'. It only got better as we got on the plane and took our seats. Once seated the fun really began. Blitz: 'We're all gonna die' as we're all laughing. Then the stewardess comes over to Johnny and says 'It'll be alright, would you like to meet the captain?' So, Johnny goes with her to the cockpit. A while later he walks back down the aisle and announces to everyone. 'It's okay everybody, I met the Captain and he's not an asshole so we're gonna be alright'.

Johnny is sitting next to me on the plane and as we're getting our meals the stewardess says 'We have some extra bottles of wine would you guys like some?' So she brings out a half dozen bottles of wine. Next thing I know Johnny accidently knocks one over and it spills right in my crotch. There have been very few times in my life that I have ever lost my temper and this was one of them. I yelled at him 'That's it, get the fuck out of here! Go to the back of the plane!' (Then I thought to myself, you know,

Frank... Blitz would probably kill you in a fight) but Johnny got up and went to the back of the plane. A minute later I here this voice just loud enough for me, Jimmy and Stiv to hear. 'Fuck all you guys... I'll take this fuckin' plane to Cuba'. We all just all busted out laughing. You've got to love that guy.

When we got to Boston I told Johnny 'Come on, I'm taking you out to dinner at this great restaurant I know in Boston called 'The Coach And Four'. They had the best prime rib and Yorkshire pudding in the country. So we went off to dinner. I love all of those guys so much. I wouldn't trade my time touring with Jimmy, Johnny, Stiv, Cheetah, George Cabaniss and David Steinberg for anything.

THE DISCONNECTED BAND, LAST BATORS TOUR 1980-81 WITH BRIAN JAMES

After Johnny Blitz left the band in the spring of 1980 we got David Quinton Steinberg to play drums with us. David had already played on our Bomp! single *Not That Way Anymore* and *Circumstantial Evidence*. This version of the band, Me, Jimmy Zero, George Cabaniss, Stiv and David would tour continuously through the spring and summer and George, David, Stiv and I would record the 'Disconnected' album in August and September. We again played the Whisky A Go-Go for 3 days, did the Uncle Floyd TV Show in Newark and toured all summer did the 'Urgh!! A Music War' west coast tour with Pere Ubu, The Members and Magazine in August. Then in late August and September we recorded the 'Disconnected' album in Sun Valley, California at Perspective Studio.

The LP was released right before John Lennon was killed in New York City. We had tour dates set and started playing in New York a week or so after. Brian James from the Damned had come over with Stiv from England and joined us for a second guitar on that tour. I remember Geoff Jones driving all of us up past the Dakota Building. There were still tons of flowers everywhere. It was so terribly sad. Our first concert was at Irving Plaza in New York then we did the Uncle Floyd Show again and played *I Had Too Much To Dream (Last Night)* and *The Last Year* and then went on tour. Our last gig was the Channel in Boston on the coldest day of the decade in January of 1981.

63

NATIONAL RECORD MART #39

One of the supremely ironic aspects of being a professional musician on the cusp of fame and success is that sometimes you'd have to take a day job to make money during the leaner times. Most of us landed in music or record stores. It was not unheard of to sell records you were on to people who had no idea you played on the record. It actually happened to me dozens of times. I supplemented my income by working at National Record Mart from March 1978 until February 1979 when I started playing with Stiv's band. I also went back there from 1982 until 1990 as a manager of the Infidels and while I was in Club Wow 1982-85.

In 1983 one afternoon two scruffy looking punks walked up to me at the counter and plopped down $10.00 and the Stiv Bators 'Disconnected' LP. I just looked at them and said 'What kind of sickos are you guys to buy crap like this?' They got offended and started defending Stiv. 'Ah, Stiv's great man.'... Then I started laughing and said turn the cover over and pointed to the upper left corner. 'That's me.' They looked at it a few moments and shook my hand and we all started to laugh. Their names were Pete Drivere and John Hlumyk and they told me they had a band called The Infidels. They asked me if I would come to hear them practice one day and give my opinion of the band. I said 'Sure'. So, a week later I ended up at Tony Mentzer's garage (Tony was their lead singer) and met Ken Laverty who was their drummer.

They ran through a number of songs including mine and Stiv's *The Last Year* and some other covers but what caught my ear was their originals *Summertime Sucks* and *Oh! Baby*. I had just finished up with Stiv Bators and had started playing in Club Wow in Cleveland. They asked me what I thought of their band and if I could help them out. I told them I'll talk to a few people and see what I can do. I called my best friend Geoff Jones and told him about the Infidels. Well they're really not too good yet (a lot of it was probably nerves and playing in an actual garage) but they think they're great. They have some great song writing ideas and are charismatic personalities and funny for teenagers. Picture the 17 year old Jim Kendzor, Frank Secich and Stiv Bators smart asses you once knew and you'll get the picture. I think one day with work and guidance they will be famous. I think they're really on to something. They're the real thing. Geoff said 'So we should work with them then?'

'Yeah, it would be a good idea'. So, Geoff Jones and I started to manage and produce The Infidels. We did that for about 8 years. Now 30 years later I'm in the Deadbeat Poets with them.

64

9:25 AND SEVEN SECONDS, WONDROUS STRANGE

I've always thought that the title of the Infidels debut album '9:25 And Seven Seconds' was one of the best album titles ever. They had a big clock in their rehearsal place and it was broken and the hands were frozen in at that time. They were clever lads. I'll continue their story from the previous paragraph. The Infidels (Pete Drivere-lead guitar, John Hlumyk-bass guitar, Tony Mentzer-vocals and Ken Laverty-drums) formed in 1982. Ken left in the fall of 1983. First recording dates were in winter of 1982/83 at Paul Pope's Yogi Recording Studio in Elyria, Ohio with me producing the songs *Summertime Sucks* and *Oh Baby*. Ken left in the fall of 1983. John Koury stepped in on drums. Second dates were in late winter of 1983/84 and final sessions were in fall of 1984 and included *Poor Little Rich Girl, It's Alright, Mad About That Girl, A Thousand Years Ago* and *I Can't Take It No More*.

1985 saw their first single *Mad About That Girl* b/w *A Thousand Years Ago* on the Jim's Records label which was also a popular record store in Pittsburgh run by Jim Spitznagel. Local DJ here named Tom Biery played the demo for Jim and it was Jim's first release. The single sold 2,000 copies which was great for an Indie release. Tony Mentzer left the band in May of 1985 and was replaced by guitarist David Lisko.

1986 saw their first seven inch EP called 'Infidels X 4', an amazing little record on Scream Records which Geoff Jones and I started. I also licensed their early recordings to the GMG label in France who put out the first Infidels 12" record 'Mad About That Girl' where it sold very well, was played all over the country and garnered critical acclaim from the French rock press.

1987 saw their first Scream Records 45 *I Can't Seem To Make You Mine* b/w *Everywhere I Go* and a national tour opening for the Dead Boys. 1988 was the Infidels first full-length LP '9:25 And Seven Seconds', 1990's Scream release of 'Wondrous Strange' was the Infidels first release on compact disc.

The Infidels were a very talented and critically acclaimed band and my one big regret and Geoff's too was that we couldn't get them signed to a major label. It wasn't for lack of trying or talent. They made wonderful classic records and we were very close to a contract at A&M. Aaron Jacoves A&M/A&R director even flew to Youngstown from LA to see them. We also did a record label showcase in New York City. It's a fickle business and even the best of artists can and do get passed by.

John and Dave left spring of '91 and Pete kept the band going as a touring performing band until 1995. The Infidels reformed in 2000 with the classic line-up John, Pete, Dave and John. They still occasionally go out and play and have played in Aruba and recently opened for Cheap Trick in San Diego, California and of course Pete Drivere, John Koury and now also John Hlumyk are Deadbeat Poets.

INSIDE OUTSIDE

(THE INFIDELS)

Tell Me Something That I Can't Understand
Tell Me Girl What You Want From A Man
I Did Everything That I Could Say And Do
I Gave All My Love And Shared It All With You

I Suppose You Could Another Man More
Is That The Reason You Kicked Me Out Your Door
I Did Everything I Could Do Or Say
But Things Just Always Seem To End That Way

You're Playing Games With My Heart
Waiting For My Tears To Start
And You're Laughing When I Cry
Walking With Some Other Guy

You Turn Me Inside Outside Upside Down
Inside Outside All Around

There's No Other Man Who Could Love You More
And That's A Fact That You Just Can't Ignore
Tell Me Girl Now How's It Going To Be
Tell Me Girl Are You Still In Love With Me

You're Playing Games With My Heart
Waiting For My Tears To Start
And You're Laughing When I Cry
Walking With Some Other Guy

I Know Exactly What's On Your Mind
You've Got Something Planned
And It's Not Very Kind
Girl I See What's Going Through Your Head
So I'm Going To Leave You Now

Before You Can Leave Me Dead

65

CLUB WOW, JIMMY ZERO – 1982-1985

On January 1st, 1982 Jimmy Zero, Jeff West and Billy Sullivan from Club Wow asked me to join the band. I was thrilled because I knew what great players and singers they were. They had already made a handful of recordings at Kirk Yano's After Dark Studio in Parma. Ohio that were really great and I was glad they asked me to be in the band. I would drive to our practice loft on St. Clair in downtown Cleveland three times a week and it was exactly 100 miles each way from my house in Sharon. I would also stay on the weekends a lot of times at Bob Kierer's apartment in Strongsville, Ohio so we could practice more. If Bob's name is familiar it's because he has been the executive producer on all the Deadbeat Poets records. I also worked a full-time job at National Record Mart and managed and produced The Infidels and I still loved every minute of it.

Club Wow was myself, Jimmy Zero (from the Dead Boys), Jeff West (from Testors) and Billy Sullivan who is currently in Herman's Hermits. Our whole goal was to get a major label deal. We usually played at the Phantasy or the Agora in Cleveland or Cedars in Youngstown or JB's in Kent. So we rehearsed and recorded a lot to record demos and only played "live" once a month. We opened up for few name bands in concert namely Meatloaf and The Lords Of The New Church.

We put out one single *Prettiest Girl* b/w *The Nights Are So Long* and that has been our only release. We recorded about 20 songs at Paul Pope's studio in Elyria, Ohio and four at Britain Square. We were together for three years and just like the Infidels we got very close to getting signed but could not pull it off. In the beginning of 1985, we went to New York and rehearsed a full week there for a big record showcase. We even add a sax player for the big show at Tracks. There were no takers.

We have about 28 well recorded songs and some great video and film footage. Club Wow was a very good live band and there are many outstanding 'live' songs like Jimmy's *The Wild Ride Of Vera Jane* about Jane Mansfield and our cover of *Strawberry Fields Forever* which is one of my favorites. All of this will finally be released by Zero Hour Records of Australia titled 'Nowhere Fast'.

Club Wow was one of my favorite bands I was ever in and one of the best kept secrets of Rock and Roll. It shouldn't have been. By the way, the original single of *The Prettiest Girl* will be available again as a bonus 45 in a beautiful picture sleeve as well to celebrate this release. It would be wonderful for all of us to get together and do a few shows to celebrate the release.

A MILLION MILES AWAY (Club Wow Version)

(Frank Secich)

You must stay behind I'm sorry it's so
It's nothing personal but you can't go
Cause I'm with the girl who's got the stuff
It's not real life but it's good enough
And I'm a million miles away
I'm a million miles away
And you can't reach me today
I'm disconnected all the way

What's the disturbance I'm eating my meal
How the hell do you know what I feel
They're playing at killing out here in the streets
When I'd give anything for a good night's sleep
But I'm a million miles away
I'm a million miles away
And you can't reach me today
I'm disconnected all the way

I think of a girl that I once had
Her face is a blank I remember her sad
She moves to the summer every Halloween
She can't understand how she died in her dream

At the war museum there's a new art show
The self-portrait of Vincent van Gogh
Of course I was there to cash in my soul
Now get me out of here before I lose control
I'm a million miles away
I'm a million miles away
And you can't reach me today
I'm disconnected all the way

66

JACOB GEOFFREY SECICH

Lisa and I had put off starting a family for 9 years as I tried so hard with her full support to make it in the music business. About the time Club Wow fell apart I was promoted to manager at National Record Mart, so we decided to start a family. The best day in my life was October 13, 1986 when my son Jacob Geoffrey Secich was born. I gave him the middle name Geoffrey because he was born on Geoff Jones' birthday. I also asked Geoff to be Jake's Godfather.

67

I'VE BEEN AWAY 1990-2003

No, I wasn't in prison but I did leave the music business. On June 4, 1990 I got a call from my old friend, Bobby Brabant, 'Frank, I have some terrible news'. I could tell by the tone of his voice what it was. I just said 'How did he die?'

I played an acoustic set for the Stiv Bators benefit at the Babylon in Cleveland that was put on by Jeff Reding for Stiv's parents in June and then played an acoustic set in Youngstown at Cedars. My friend, Beaver Warner died four days later on June, 8, 1990.

I decided to quit the music business. I just walked away. I resigned from National Record Mart. I got another job and didn't even touch a guitar for the next 13 years. I had a young three year old son, Jacob and I decided to spend a lot of my time with him growing up which my dad never got to do with me. Once a week we'd go on a fun day together and with my new job I was home every night. I really didn't miss the music business all that much. I became a Little League coach and a hockey coach. I got a job with an insurance company and became a manager then a district manager.

I loved being there watching Jake grow up. I never missed a baseball or hockey game. He became a very good hockey player and played on teams year round and we went to many tournaments all over Canada, Michigan, New York, Ohio and all around. It was nice too because when he played in Canada my old friend David Quinton Steinberg always came to see him play and we got to hang out together. He played until he went to college. Jacob graduated from Slippery Rock University with honors and lives and works in the Bellevue area of Pittsburgh. I couldn't be more proud of him.

Sometime in 2003, for the first in 13 years I picked up my 1966 Gibson guitar (with 13 year old strings) and started playing and this great guitar riff came from nowhere. I thought 'Shit, now I'm going to have to write this thing'. In twenty minutes I had it finished exactly how you read it here.

The songs just started pouring out of me. The tears had poured out long ago.

THE STIV BATORS GHOST TOUR

(Frank Secich)

On Youngstown's north side tour I saw
On Wick Avenue
A car surfer hanging ten in front
Of Ursuline high school
Hey! Hey! Stiv Bators
Are you listening?
Are you laughing?

On Toronto's ghost tour I saw
Yonge Street's snow and slush
And a pretty woman wearing a mink coat
About to get a rush
Hey! Hey! Stiv Bators
Swilling Carlsberg
Are you driving then?

On Cleveland's ghost tour I saw
On Euclid Avenue
A leather kid with drunken sun-glassed eyes
Who looked up just like you
Hey! Hey! Stiv Bators
Do "Junebug" for us, one more
time singin'
"Ain't No Sunshine When She's
Gone"

On New York's ghost tour I saw
Cheetah, Johnny, Jimmy and you
Shakin' up that sleepy orange-lit world
With nothin' to do
Hey! Hey! Stiv's hanging
Off a fire escape in St. Mark's Place

Whoa..
On LA's ghost tour I saw
The very Sunset Strip
Kim Fowley, Rodney
and Greg Shaw
Wasn't that a trip?
Hey! Hey! Stiv Bators
Are you staying or are you off
again?

On London's ghost tour I saw
Some graffiti on Savile Row
Of a blind-folded girl watching
Truffaut's
"The 400 Blows"
Hey! Hey! Stiv Bators
At the beach by the sea
Well practically

On the Paris ghost tour I saw
You knocked to the street and
Brush it off as nothing and walk
home
To sleep it off and dream
Hey! Hey! Stiv Bators
If you see Rimbaud
Tell him I said "Hello"

JENNYBURG HILL

(Frank Secich)

I'm going to go back to Jennyburg Hill
In my mind with you on a Saturday afternoon
Maybe in March or better May still
Just once for a good laugh like we used to do
High on Prospect Heights
Overlooking the town
I hear the New York train
& the traffic sounds
As the day goes down

I'm going to go back to Jennyburg Hill
Sit on the checkered wall & with some Wild I (Irish Rose)
Up against it all then, I joked with my friends but then
I could always make you laugh, now couldn't I
The whistle ends the shift
Workers hitting the bars (like the Bar Haiti on Broadway)
Just like clockwork at 8:00 AM
For breakfast & beer

Here's to a long time ago when time stood still up
On Jennyburg Hill

A fist fight outside of the Maennerchor Club
A crowd gathers around
Some things never change
Around Orchard Street
The river flows on below Jennyburg Hill moving on it's way

The pavement cracks where the grass grows through the
asphalt grey
Reminds me of you & yesterday but in a good way

And as the sun sets on Jennyburg Hill
I gather some good thoughts to head on back home
Over streets I know well where they say not to go anymore,
anyway
Here's to a long time ago where time stood still
Up On Jennyburg Hill

68

MARK HERSHBERGER, AROUND AGAIN AND POP DETECTIVE

The only reason the Frank Secich story has a better ending than it would have and you are now reading about it is a man named Mark Hershberger. During my hiatus as an insurance salesman from 1990-2003 he went through great lengths in the 1990's to track me down for an interview with me for a Blue Ash article he was doing under his Pop Detective moniker for Audities Magazine. In 1996, Mark did an in depth article on Blue Ash that's still one of the best articles on us ever. Mark started out as a musician in the Allentown area with 'The Few' 1980-82 and 'Agency' 1982-92. As a diehard Blue Ash fan it was his idea to not let this music or Blue Ash's legacy die. He wanted to archive and release some of the rare studio recordings and demos that he knew were languishing in a huge box at Peppermint Productions in Youngstown. He contacted me in 2003 and I then went to Peppermint Productions to visit Gary Rhamy and take stock of what Blue Ash recordings that were there. To my great surprise Gary had saved everything and we started taking inventory. We found 219 recordings. I was shocked and stunned. Mark was delighted.

In 2003, he ran the idea past Bruce Brodeen at Not Lame recordings who persuaded Mark to let him do it as he already had the knowledge of putting such things out. He was also instrumental in hooking Blue Ash up with IPO head David Bash and we were booked to play our first gig in 25 years for the International Pop Overthrow at the Khyber Club in Philadelphia. Blue Ash's 'Around Again (Rarities From The Vault 1972-79)' was released in 2004 with Mark writing the liner notes. During the Blue Ash reunion shows Mark turned up at every one of the gigs.

When the Deadbeat Poets formed in 2006 and we started recording and Mark was ready to launch his record label and dream. Mark's first proper release on Pop Detective Records would be the Deadbeat Poets' debut 'Notes From The Underground' in June of 2007. That summer, the album got rave reviews and most notably was rave reviewed not once but twice in USA Today. Our first gig was at Goldmine Magazine's National Record Convention at the Rock and Roll Hall of Fame in Cleveland. Pop Detective and the Deadbeat Poets were off and running. Since then the Pop Detective moniker can be found on great releases by the Dahlmanns, Deadbeat Poets, Sexie Heroes, Vibeke Saugestad, The Go Wows, The Jellybricks, Saturday City. The

Terrifieds and the Yum Yums.

Mark has now had 26 releases on Pop Detective which have yielded 14 'Coolest Songs In The World' on Little Steven's Underground Garage nationally syndicated show and untold air play on Sirius XM. His artist roster alone makes Pop Detective one of the premier Indie labels in America.

Go to popdetective.com and check out the goodies and buy something actually "Made In America" and brought to you by a true American entrepreneur.

What more can I say about him? Oh yeah, he's the only person in the world who has both shaken Queen Elizabeth's hand and actually owns one of Buddy Holly's neckties.

69

DEADBEAT POETS – A NEW BEGINNING

I asked two of my old friends Pete Drivere and Tom Sailor who both had studios if I could come in when they both had some extra time (which they were kind to give me) and lay down some acoustic tracks of new songs that I had written just to hear what they sounded like on tape: *The Stiv Bators Ghost Tour, A Funny Little Feeling, The Green Man, The Black Light Room, Madras Man (A Blues In 3/4 Time)* and others. After Greg Shaw died in October of 2004, Patrick and Suzy from Bomp! Records got a hold of me and asked if I'd get a bunch of Ohio musicians together and do a track for the upcoming tribute album they were putting together for Greg. I got together Pete and John from The Infidels, Dave Swanson from Rainy Day Saints, David 'Quinton' Steinberg, George Cabaniss, Jimmy Zero, Billy Sullivan and Bill Bartolin to record at Ampreon Recorder which is Pete's studio in Youngstown.

The album and companion book were called 'He Put The Bomp!' I picked *Him Or Me (What's It Gonna Be?)* by Paul Revere & The Raiders to record for Greg's tribute. Pete, John, Bill and I played on the track. All the rest of us sang on it. Everyone did a line or two. It came off very well. Anyway, I really loved the sound we made. I thought if I decide to record my new songs that this would be the band I'd use. I also decided that if I record again I'd want my old friend Terry Hartman in the band. It took me a while to find Hartman. He had disappeared just like me. Finally, one of his sons was recording at Pete's and Pete got his number for me.

I called Terry and asked him to be in the band. So the band kind of accidentally formed. As I've mentioned before Terry is one of the great songwriters to ever come from Ohio but few people knew of him. The Deadbeat Poets cut two songs at Ampreon *The Truth About Flying Saucers* and *A Funny Little Felling*. Bill 'Cupid' Bartolin also played guitar on both of these recordings. I sent these songs along with my acoustic demos to Patrick Boissel at Alive Records. He really liked them but said that was not the kind of thing his label was doing. He gave a lead to a Japanese label that he thought would love it. I then sent off all these songs to Haruko Shiozawa at Vivid Sound Records in Japan and 12 hours later she offered us a recording contract.

We then recorded our first album 'Notes From The Underground' which was later released in Japan. In the meanwhile we released it here as the debut release on Pop

Detective Records. The Deadbeat Poets were in business.

70

BLUE ASH REUNIONS AND REISSUES 2003 – 2009

So the original Blue Ash line-up (Frank Secich, Bill Bartolin, David Evans, Jim Kendzor and with the addition of Bobby Darke on bass) played our first gig at the Khyber Club in Philadelphia for David Bash's International Pop Overthrow. I played rhythm guitar on all the reunion gigs. Stewkie's Nazz was also on the bill and we had a great time hanging with him, Mark Hershberger and Ken Sharp the writer. We did a fun set and ended it with a cover of Badfinger's *Baby Blue*.

In August of 2004 Bruce Brodeen and Not Lame Recordings released the Blue Ash retrospective 'Around Again (A Collection Of Rarities From The Vault 1972-79)' which contained 44 never before released recordings by Blue Ash from the Peppermint Studio archives. It was a limited edition and sold out several presssings and is very rare and the cheapest you can find it on Amazon UK is £108.33. It will be re-released as part of the Zero Hour Records Australia Blue Ash Box Set in 2016, so it will be available soon again with about 80 more rare of the rarest Blue Ash songs.

Our next gig would be Blue Ash CD release party in August of 2004 at the B&B Backstage 2004 in Youngstown with Mountain and Vanilla Fudge. That was fun because in addition our second drummer Jeff Rozniata joined us for that show splitting drumming and singing duties with David Evans and also Brian Wingrove our piano player came on board as well. The highlight of the show was Sean Bartolin (Bill and Darla's son) sitting in with us on guitar and taking the solo on *Tired of Pushing*. His solo brought the house down and Bill beamed with pride and looked over at me on stage and said 'Sean's better than me'. B&B Backstage is a great outdoor venue and tons of our fans came to see us and we partied with everyone after the concert and signed CD's and reminisced. Bruce 'Bowie' McNeeledge our old roadie and friend came all the way from Arizona wearing his 30 year old Blue Ash T-shirt. People came to see us from all over the country. It was really something else seeing everyone again and it was all filmed as well. We also played a few more concerts in 2004: The Corinthian Ballroom in Sharon, PA with guest stars The Infidels on the bill and at the Beachland Ballroom in Cleveland where I met up with my old friend Jimmy Zero who I hadn't seen in almost 20 years.

Blue Ash didn't play anymore reunion dates until 2008 when Collectors Choice reissued 'No More, No Less' for the first time on CD. It was a huge success and just like the original release was rave reviewed everywhere. It was even in the New York Daily News (Sunday Edition) as the lead off review. Which was amazing for an LP that had been out of print for 35 years. It also topped the Amazon Power Pop chart at #1 for a few weeks and was listed in Rolling Stone as one of the Top Ten selling CD's in New York City in an October issue and Blue Ash was featured in a 5 page full color article and spread by Christopher Duda in the Shindig Magazine in the UK in 2008. It was nice to finally get all the recognition. I was so glad it happened before Bill left us. I think he got the biggest kick out of it. We played for the International Pop Overthrow in Youngstown on November 15, 2008 to a wild and crazy crowd in our hometown.

Blue Ash played in January of 2009 at the Barrow Civic Theater in Franklin on a night of one of the worst snowstorms of the decade. My old friend Neal Williams had put on the show and we had our old friend Max Schang opening. I still can't get over how many people came out to see us in that blizzard. It was truly touching. The last Blue Ash gig ever would be March 21, 2009 at the Corinthian Ballroom for the Billy Dach Benefit in Sharon, PA. That would be the last Blue Ash gig ever. We were set to tour Canada in the summer of 2009 but had to cancel. Bill Bartolin fell ill and was diagnosed with cancer in early September. Bill died on October 3, 2009.

71

ON THE ROAD WITH THE DEADBEAT POETS – 2008

The year 2008 started off with a bang for the Deadbeat Poets. We were invited to play the esteemed SXSW Festival in Austin in March. So Pete Drivere, Bob Kierer, John Koury, Terry Hartman and myself decided to drive rather than fly and stop and see all the sights. After driving all night and the next day we found ourselves in Mexia, Texas (Home of Anna Nicole Smith which many a town folk person will tell you she used to work in the fast food chicken place down the road) which is right down the road from Wortham where Blind Lemon Jefferson is buried. Wortham is 8 miles north of Mexia on Rt.14. We decided to pay our respects the next morning.

The SXSW festival is quite an event. There are showcases, concerts and venues all over Austin, Our slot was at Lambert's Patio which is a fabulous barbecue place and they had a stage set up outside under a huge tent. There are tens of thousands of people attending the festival as well as the native population of Austin. The Austin Chronicle had given our album 'Notes From The Underground' us a great review in the newspaper which surprised us and helped a lot to get people to see us. Kent Benjamin, a writer from Austin had been instrumental in getting us to play SXSW and I hung out with him and went to a lot of venues which was cool. The next night , my old friend Eddy Best who lives in Austin came down and we went out to a bunch of venues as well and had a great time.

In May of 2008 we were headed off the UK to play the International Pop Overthrown Festival in Liverpool and to play in Scotland. Mark Hershberger had also got our song *No Island Like The Mind, No Ship Like Beer* played at the Liverpool Football Club games at Anfield Stadium

Playing the Cavern and just being in Liverpool was a trip. We played in the afternoon at the Cavern Pub which is across the street from the club which we then played in the evening for the International Pop Overthrow Liverpool. We went over great and it was unreal like a dream. Afterward, I called my wife Lisa from a cell phone on Matthew Street outside the Cavern. 'We just got an encore and standing ovation at the Cavern. I'm a little overwhelmed but I had to call you'.

A Scotsman named Brian Barry walked up to me on the street introduced himself and his partner Jacqui 'We're big fans and have spent a thousand pounds to take our holiday this week to come to Liverpool and hang out with you here'. I said, 'Brian, if you're that crazy... We're going to wind up being great friends'. Which we did and we are.

On the Saturday morning we had off, I woke John and Pete at 6:00am from the apartment we had rented in the Cornwallis Apartments (I couldn't wake Bob and Terry) as they had been out drinking at the Blue Angel until 3:00am. I said 'Come on we're going on the Beatles tour' which I had all mapped out. We got bus passes for the day and we caught a bus near Lime St. Station and headed out to 251 Menlove Ave. at 7:00am. Being a Saturday there was hardly anyone on bus so we sat up front and talked to the driver. He said, 'I'll drop you off right in front of Aunt Mimi's house'. We called Chris Leonardi (our keyboardist on all our recordings and huge Beatles fan) at 9:00am and woke him up at 4:00am Ohio time. 'We 're at 'Strawberry Field' 'You woke me up at 4:00am to tell me that?'. We proceeded down Church St. to St. Peter's Church where Paul McCartney first met John Lennon on July 6, 1957 at the church fete. There was a small cemetery next to the church where a few folks were tending to the graves of their loved ones on a beautiful sunny May morning. I started chatting with a couple named Jack and Mona. Jack: 'Are you guys checking out all the Beatles sights?' Me: 'Yeah'. Jack: 'Have you been to Mimi's house yet?' Me: 'Yeah, we went there first'. Jack: 'Then you know that "Working Class Hero" was a bunch of bollocks?' (Mimi's old house on Menlove Ave, is in a very nice neighborhood with a golf course across the street. It's by no means a working class area). Me: 'Then we went to Strawberry Field and now here', Looking over the field by the church I said. 'I would think from photos I've seen that the Quarrymen played right back there by the hedgerow?' Jack: 'You're close it was about 40 feet to the left'. Me: 'Don't tell me you were here that day?' Jack: 'Yeah, I was. I was 10 years old. This was our church'. 'Are you guys a band?' Me: 'Yeah. We're called the Deadbeat Poets and we're playing here at the Cavern and just got back from playing in Scotland'. Jack: 'Deadbeat Poets?' You have the football song?' Me: 'Yeah, that's us'. Then a very nice lady named Jean joined in the conversation Jean: 'Have you seen the graves, yet?' I said 'No, what graves? She took us down a row of tombstones and showed us the Eleanor Rigby headstone and a few down from that the MacKenzie headstone. Then Jean said 'Paul and John actually didn't meet outside when the Quarrymen played they met later in the day inside this building when they played later on' Me: 'You were here too that day, Jean? Jean: 'Yes'.

We ate lunch in a cafe in the Woolton Village proper then headed for Penny Lane and spent the afternoon there in music stores and record shoppes. As we were walking down Penny Lane, I said to Pete 'Look there's Dovedale Primary School where both John Lennon and George Harrison attended. All the street signs for Penny Lane were all painted black and white instead of the regular metal street signs that are all over Liverpool. I asked a merchant about it and he said 'They used to replace them all the time because as soon as the signs were put up they'd be stolen as souvenirs so now all the Penny Lane signs are painted on.

Later that evening we boarded the Mersey River Ferry to Birkenhead along with 600 others and when all were aboard a voice comes over the loudspeakers 'Ladies and gentlemen welcome aboard the world famous Mersey River Ferry' then you hear Gerry and the Pacemakers sing *Life goes on day after day*......... It was truly very cool. Getting off at the ferry station in Birkenhead we walked two blocks up the hill and entered the first pub we saw. The Worsley Arms.

We were very hungry and asked if they served food. They said only sandwiches so we decided to leave and find a restaurant. Then a voice called out 'You're missing out on one of the finest pub experiences in all the North of England.' Then me (not one to miss out on one of the finest pub experiences in all the North of England) said to the guys 'I'll stay here just pick me up on your way back' and they left. 'Okay, Yank there's just one question before we get started with this event. (I'm thinking... What fuckin' event?). 'Of what political party do you belong to? (I'm thinking... Oh, here we go). 'In America, I'm a Democrat. Over here I guess that would be the equivalent to your Labour Party' (applause from the pub customers). 'Good fookin' answer, if it would have been the other you would have been thrown out in the street on your arse'. More laughter then silence for a moment then me 'We'll it would have taken more than the three of YOU to do it'. Dead silence............... 'What would you like to drink, Yank?... And bring him some food as well'. The three introduced themselves as John, Chuck and Dave. The owner and the patrons wouldn't let me pay for a thing all night as we argued at length: Baseball vs Cricket.(I won) US Football vs Soccer or their football (a tie nil nil), American Guinness vs Proper Guinness (they won) and the differences...... As I drank nine 20oz pints of it that night and I was three sheets to the wind. It's much stronger than the American Guinness we have. We laughed all night and cajoled each other as only truly drunken louts can do. When the guys came back to pick me up 3 hours later, Terry took one look at me and said 'I knew that was a bad idea leaving you here'.

72

CIRCUSTOWN

We would spend most of 2009 working on our second album Circustown. I first mention it in Madras Man (A Blues In 3/4 Time) and Terry wrote his epic closing song *Circustown* for the album which sums it all up. Circustown is a real place near Butler, Pa about 50 miles southeast of where I live. Circustown is a haunting place. I first discovered it 30 years ago; Most of the buildings still survive. According to what I could find out it was built after turn of the century around 1910-1915. It was a permanent summer carnival/circus/zoo built by Pittsburgh industrialists and steel magnates. They would put the poor children of their workers on trains from the slums of Pittsburgh and send them to a rural railway siding that is still at Circustown. It would give them a one-day vacation out in the country air with animals, rides, games and a good meal. There is precious little about it on the internet, so I don't really know the true story, just what I've heard. It's now an abandoned ruin in a field.

The photo on the cover of the CD booklet is a fairly recent actual photo of it. There are two different stories about why it closed down. One is that the depression came in the 1930's and it was no longer feasible and the other is that a gorilla killed a kid. There are about 30 buildings still standing. The main one is on the cover of the booklet. My son, Jacob took that photograph. The buildings are all made of corrugated steel & painted a burgundy color. They are rusting badly now. The sideshow tents are made steel and tin and look like Arabian tents and are nestled up and down the huge field. It is an unbelievably surreal place. I go there occasionally and can spend hours there. It just exudes Americana. I always thought it would be a great title for an album. In a strange way, it mirrors much of the area I grew up in like Youngstown and Western Pennsylvania. It is a sad, wonderful, magical place. I have heard lately that is has been bulldozed over but I don't know since I haven't been there for a few years so at least we have the photographs and the music.

THE POSTMODERN RAZOR WIRE SHOWDOWN

(Frank Secich)

A smiling blonde, contortionist
Had my number, with every twist
Letting her hair down
We locked in a stare down
Over a suitcase
Filled with cliches
But she couldn't pronounce my name
Then she addressed me in German &
In a menacing way

Spoke of the current world economic slowdown
(and the price of eggs)
At the postmodern razor wire showdown

In a rather pedestrian
Somewhat equestrian
Riotous, bellicose, symbolic howl
I drew my revolver
The great problem solver &
Rode into the gunfight
At the OK Corral
I saw Wyatt Earp & Doc Holiday
In every direction, I fired away

I put on my shades & slowly watched it go down (into the melting ground)
At the Postmodern razor wire showdown

I hear the rebels are comin'
They're armed & annoyed
To be doing the dozens with
Pretty Boy Floyd
I could not believe
The dilemma this posed
When the crowd turned mean
As the flea market closed

I walked right into John Butler Train
"I ain't marchin' no more" was all he would say
Then the Stetson's & Fedoras were all thrown down (outside the gates)
Of the postmodern razor wire showdown

I jabbed with my left
Threw a round house right
Figured that I was ready to fight
But I turned around as I heard the sound
Of broken blossoms hitting the ground

I saw a young girl in a mirror
Silent & falling as I was drawing nearer
To the one conclusion I could draw from this commotion (in a haze of brown)
At the postmodern razor wire showdown

One day at a Deadbeat Poets Circustown recording session in 2010, I picked up a 12-string that was laying about and started playing and singing this song. Pete looks over to me and says 'What is that song?' I said 'It's a song I wrote along time ago in 1967. I wrote about an old girlfriend of mine named Mary Jean. Pete looked at me and said in his producer's voice 'Well, we're doing that one'.

I THOUGHT I KNEW YOU

(Frank Secich)

Don't know what hit me, it happened so fast
I went through the ceiling, came down with a crash
I thought I knew you but I thought wrong
I thought I knew you
I guess I didn't know you at all

I really thought that, I thought that I knew
& then you told me, you're sorry it's true
I thought I knew you but I thought wrong
I thought I knew you, I guess I didn't know you at all

I used to think I knew you well
But I couldn't tell
Because the things that you would say
Were so strange & very vague so far away

Now when I see you
It doesn't affect me
Maybe that's not true
But it's better that way
I thought I knew you but I thought wrong
I thought I knew you but I guess I didn't know you at all

73

COOLEST SONG IN THE WORLD – JULY 12 2010

One of the great things about being in a band and making records is that you get to meet and know some very interesting and special people. I had the great pleasure over the internet of making the acquaintance of Robbie Duke/Patrick Pink who was the last person ever recorded by the legendary Joe Meek and was there at Joe's tragic death. I had written *The Staircase Stomp!* about Joe Meek who was one of my all-time heroes.

After the Deadbeat Poets recorded it, I sent Robbie a copy and was so honored that he liked it. Our big break came when *The Staircase Stomp!* was picked as "Coolest Song in The World" July 12, 2010 on Little Steven's Underground Garage which is broadcast weekly and is nationally and internationally syndicated on over 250 stations in North America and all over Europe in addition to being broadcast on Voice Of America in over 50 countries and Armed Forces Radio. It is a hugely popular radio show heard by millions. We were on the national show for eight weeks and on heavy rotation and a hit on Sirius XM. It was later in the year voted by the worldwide listeners of the show as #5 "Coolest Song in The World 2010". The really strange thing about the song is that when Pete was done mixing it, we played it back. It had a very haunting vibe. Then it hit me! I said "Pete, Oh My God today is February 3rd." That was the day that Buddy Holly died in 1959 and Joe Meek and Violet Shenton died in 1967.

THE STAIRCASE STOMP

(Secich)

Calling Buddy Holly on the Ouija board
Should I use a major to a minor chord?
The furniture is dancing in the psycho ward
I hear a new world that I'm headed toward

Calling into Brian on the Dictaphone
Do you come here often when you're all alone?
Popping diet pills & bouncing off the walls
Talking to a cat at the Warley Lee farm

Stomp! Stomp! Stomp!
Do the staircase stomp
Rock! Rock! Rock!
Until we drop
In those magic spinning reels
There were tragic turning wheels &
The passion that kills

Calling up to Telstar out in space
The sound of the future falling right in place
The Syndicats blasting Crawdaddy Simone
The rockin' beat of the Honeycombs

But there were hidden microphones in the wallpaper
Decca & Spector have their spies everywhere
Rent boys & paranoia, bills in hand
Debt & depression took a hold of the man

Stomp! Stomp! Stomp!
Do the staircase stomp
Rock! Rock! Rock!
Until we drop
In those magic spinning reels
There were tragic turning wheels &
The passion that kills

It was February 3rd on Holloway Road
Joe was staring at the unopened mail
Joe turned to Patrick asking if he would
Go down & get Violet, if you'd be so good

Hey Joe where you going with that gun in your hand?
Patrick heard some shouting & a big, loud bang
Violet fell down the stairs into Patrick's arms
Eight years from the day that Buddy Holly died
There's was to be a murder/suicide

Stomp! Stomp! Stomp!
Do the staircase stomp
Rock! Rock! Rock!
Until we drop
In those magic spinning reels
There were tragic turning wheels and
The passion that kills

74

YOUNGSTOWN VORTEX SUTRA (THE BRITISH VERSION)

In 2011 we released our 3rd album 'Youngstown Vortex Sutra (The British Version)' and in addition we released 'A Deadbeat Christmas' a four song EP of original Christmas music which is a perennial favorite featuring John Koury's magnificent *Christmastime In Painesville* and we also pulled another 'Coolest Song In The World' with *The Man With The X-Ray Eyes* which came in like *The Staircase Stomp!* as #5 'Coolest Song In The World 2011' on Little Steven's Underground Garage. 2012 saw the release of our critically acclaimed 4th album 'American Stroboscope' and our first video 'Who's Hieronymus Bosch And Why Is He Saying These Terrible Things About Me?' Which was picked up by video channels all over the world.

75

EUROPEAN TOUR 2012

On January 9, 2012 the Deadbeat Poets took off for our second European Tour. We flew from Pittsburgh via Toronto and Dusseldorf and landed in Prague the Czech Republic. We'd start the first leg of our tour opening for New York Junk and Phil Shoenfelt and Southern Cross there. We started off playing at a great place called Malostranska Beseda in Prague. We had a great crowd and went over well. Someone yelled from the audience 'I'm from Newton Falls' which is right near Youngstown. He came after the show and introduced himself. His name was Mark Baker and he was an author for Fodor's Guides and National Geographic and living in Prague. This kind of thing would happen at almost every city on the tour.

The next day, January 13th we got in the big touring van that Phil and Southern Cross had an headed for Dresden, Germany. They took us on the scenic route through the Sudetenland. What beautiful country we travelled through. I'd watch Cynthia from the side of the stage in places like Tante Ju in Dresden and just marvel at the fact that we're still playing and having a great time. Who would ever have thought back in 1977 we'd be in Germany doing this today. Our next stop was the Bassy Cowboy Club in Berlin on Saturday, January 14. Again a wild, appreciative crowd for all three bands. On Sunday the 15th we split off from New York Junk and Phil Shoenfelt and were on our own. We rented a car in Berlin and drove to Hamburg to play that night. We were opening for the Vibrators from England at Hafenklang in the St. Pauli District. As soon as I saw Nigel Bennett from the Vibrators at the club I recognized him from somewhere. He came up to me and said 'I know you from somewhere'. We talked for a while then he told me he was a member of The Members back in 1980 and I said 'Yeah, that's it'. When I played with Stiv Bators we did the west coast 'Urgh! A Music War Tour' together. Hamburg was one of my fave gigs of the tour.

We had only one day off on the tour so we decided to stay in Hamburg and get a hotel right on the Reeperbahn and take in all the Beatles haunts which was great. We visited all the old Beatles hang outs on and around the große freiheit: The Indra, Kaiserkeller, Top Ten and even the police station on the Reeperbahn where Pest Best, Paul McCartney and George Harrison were deported from Germany in late 1960. We couldn't find a place to park our car so John Koury went in and asked the cops where we could park and they told us to park for the night in the police parking lot. They were nice guys.

The next day we took off through the length of Germany again to the Czech Republic to play again in Prague at Chapeau Rouge opening for Lo Dost which was also a great show. Then it was off to Germany again to Chemnitz which was formerly Karl-Marx-Stadt in the former GDR (East Germany) where we played at a fantastic place called 'Subway To Peter' which was run by a cool owner named Mario who also manufactured a Garlic Liqueur of which he gave us bottles which were promptly stolen from us in Sweden. We made friends with cool German lady named Eva Liebmann when we played Dresden and she was there to see us again in Chemnitz. She was going to take us after the gig to see the famous statue of Karl Marx's head that weighs 40 tons but it was already 2:30am and we had to drive all night to catch a train in Berlin at 9:00am. Karl's fat head has to wait until our next trip and Eva promised she will take us there.

Coming up would be the craziest and zaniest day of the tour. Like I said we started driving from Chemnitz on the Czech border and got to the airport station at Berlin just in time. We went by train to the main Berlin Station then boarded a train to Copenhagen, Denmark. We had to play in Helsingborg, Sweden that night. So we leave Berlin and travel to Hamburg where we switched trains. We were supposed to go straight over land to Copenhagen or at least I thought so much when I bought our tickets before we left America. As I looked at the map we were heading north east toward Lubeck on the Baltic Sea. I thought WTF! A gentleman from Liverpool sitting in our car said to me 'Are we going to the right place?' Finally, I found a German conductor who spoke good English and asked him what was up? He said 'We had two trains leaving Hamburg for Copenhagen around the same time. One goes by land and one by sea. You are going by sea'. I said 'Okay, then we get on another train in Denmark that goes to Copenhagen?' 'Oh No, we pull the whole train on the ferry', I said 'You've got to be shitting me?' 'No' he says 'You'll love it, at Puttgarden the entire train will board the ferry and you can go up and have drinks and dinner whatever you like for an hour and a half then the train will disembark at Rodby, Denmark and continue to Copenhagen'. I never thought such a thing existed but look it up on google: 'Boat Train From Puttgarden to Rodby'.

Anyway, we finally arrive in Copenhagen around 6:00pm as promised to get a connecting train to Malmo, Sweden. We were supposed to connect to a train to Malmo but delays kept coming up on the schedule board 10 minutes then half an hour, then an hour then they made an announcement in Danish and our train had been cancelled due to an electrical problem. Meanwhile over in Sweden our friend Lars was waiting at the station with our rental car. As John Koury was the driver in Germany and the Czech Republic, I would drive in Scandinavia. I struck up a conversation with a Swedish lady in the Copenhagen Station and she had to get to Malmo where she lived as well. I told her we were a band and about our plight. I said could we just take a cab and she 'No, that would cost you $500.00', She said 'There is one way but we're going to have to go on the Copenhagen subway make two changes and get to the airport then catch the last shuttle train Malmo'. She said 'So, come on Deadbeat Poets, let's run' and we literally ran following her carrying our guitars and luggage. 'Don't worry about paying the subway, Deadbeat Poets. We don't have time. Just jump the turnstiles'. Which we did and just caught the shuttle to Malmo as it was about to pull away. We arrived at the Malmo Central Station 3 hours late and our good friend Lars Wenker was still there waiting for us. We ran to get the car and I drove like a maniac all through Malmo and it's suburbs on the highway to Helsingborg. We pulled up to our venue the Metalbar At Tivoli just as our host band the South Harbor Ringers (who are a great band) were just finishing.

So after 21 straight hours of travelling and no sleep the night before we jumped on stage and had one of our best performances of our tour to a wild and energetic crowd. We left Helsingborg to be house guests of my friend Lars Wenker in Malmo. The whole two weeks we had been in Europe the weather was beautiful and sunny, no snow and in the high 30's in January, the minute we left Malmo for Stockholm 350 miles away our luck changed and it started snowing and snowing and snowing. I was driving on the Scandinavian leg of the tour. Normally the trip from Malmo to Stockholm would take 5 hours. It took 11 hours through the most God awful conditions imaginable with only one lane usable on the superhighway we arrived in Stockholm just in time to play at the New Bowl Center Gullmarsplan with the Coroners and our friends Stupidity who had both already played.

The New Bowl Center Gullmarsplan was a surreal place. Our friends Stupidity (Tommy Sjostrom, Erniz, PA and Miss Anna) had been our guests the previous July 1st in Youngstown at Cedars while they were touring America. Stupidity is a great band and returned the favor by booking us with them in Stockholm. At the bowl center the stage was half way down the bowling lanes in the middle and spanned about 4 lanes. Bowling balls rolled under us and crashed into pins. People who bowled would watch the bands as well as stand behind to see. There was also a balcony filled with people and a restaurant off to the right of the stage. We'd never seen anything like it. What a great gig. Barbara Gunter Bröndum and Lars Bröndum came down to see us. Barbara is from Boardman, Ohio and Lars is a composer who went to Dana School Of Music in Youngstown.

Barbara also captured a few songs of ours on film that night. Our friends Stupidity also introduced us to Ed O'Neill who is a famous radio personality on Rocket Radio 95.3 Stockholm. After the gig we were honored to be house guests for the next two days of Erniz and his wife, Latte Lundqvist and son Mats who along with Tommy

Sjöström and Eva Häggmark showed us the sights of Stockholm. We ended the tour by flying home from Stockholm to New York with a drunken Finnish hockey team.

76

JOHNNY SINCERE – HALLELUJAH ANYWAY 2013-2014 AND STRANGE TALES

In July of 2013, The Deadbeat Poets shot out second video *Johnny Sincere* with Chris Rutushin filming and Todd Stanton editing. It was released to help promote our first single on Pop Detective of the same name. In the first week of December of 2013 *Johnny Sincere* was picked as our 3rd 'Coolest Song In The World' on Little Steven's Underground Garage. *Johnny Sincere* finished second behind only Joan Jett's *Any Weather* as Coolest Song In The World 2013 as voted by the world-wide fans of the show. The Deadbeat Poets spent most of 2014 recording our sixth album 'Hallelujah Anyway' which was released on Pop Detective Records in November of that year. It was also the Deadbeat Poets first album release on vinyl as well as CD.

THE CONCRETE COWS OF MILTON KEYNES

(Frank Secich & Robbie Duke)

The concrete cows of Milton Keynes
Motionlessly grazing on the green
Same blank looks on every face
The concrete cows well know their place

The concrete cows of Milton Keynes
Still they're standing still all day
The time and tide don't get in the way of
The Concrete Cows of Milton Keynes

The Concrete Cows of Milton Keynes
Pictured in the news again
You couldn't lift them with a crane
You couldn't tip them with a train

Americans we have plastic deer &
Carved & painted wooden bears
Rebel generals set in stone
Wooden Indians at cigar stores

We once had 3 foot lawn jockeys
Holding lanterns in black face
They now have faces painted tan
Where pink flamingos used to stand

Giant boys with hamburgers
Roadside touchdown Saviours
That's what we have nowadays
Where have you gone Ira Hayes?

I went there with a Fodor's Guide
To get to see them finally
But the cows were off to Italy
Lent to them for the Venice Biennale

Bought some mini concrete cows
Brought them home as souvenirs
To show my friends and to amaze
What have you done Woody Hayes

MODERN MOVERS AND SHAKERS

I like to end with a big shout out to modern movers and shakers and innovators who stick their necks out and put their money, talents, time, knowledge, good taste and best of all themselves on the radio and to those who are still crazy enough and love rock and roll enough put out records and start their own labels.

Mark Hershberger Pop Detective Records
www.popdetective.com

Steven Van Zandt and Little Steven's Underground Garage nationally syndicated radio programme and Sirius XM Channel 21
www.undergroundgarage.com

Bob Kierer Executive Producer Deadbeat Poets

John Cavanagh's "Soundwave" out of Glasgow, Scotland
www.johncavanagh.co.uk

Pedro Vizcaino You Are The Cosmos
www.youarethecosmos.com

Lars Wenker Sweden Pop Diggers
http://popdiggers.com

Oscar Garcia Kick Out The Jams
http://kotjrecords.blogspot.com

Deirdre Gilmartin "The Independent Stage" from New Jersey and around the world
https://www.facebook.com/TheIndependentStage

Roger "Twiggy" Day "Home Of Uncool Radio"
www.rogerday.co.uk

Jim Prell The Music Authority
http://cp.usa7.fastcast4u.com:2199/start/jamprell

Viking Jim and The Homegrown Show WNCD 93.3 FM The Wolf Youngstown, Ohio
www.933fmthewolf.com

Palmyra Delran Sirius XM DJ And Rock Star
Sunday Mornings 8:00 Am -12:00 PM
www.sirius.com Channel 21

Patryick Albert Le Havre, France
rockencaux.musicblog.fr

Bill Kelly "Teenage Wasteland" WFMU
https://wfmu.org/blackhole/main.html

Carl Cafarelli
Dana And Carl "This is Rock And Roll Radio"
https://www.facebook.com/pages/This-is-Rock-n-Roll-Radio/61791922549

Howard Byrne- Power Pop Stew
www.powerpopstew.com

Radio New York International With Dave Boogieman and Barry The Badman
www.johnlightning.com/ with Dave Kaufman & Barry Dreyfus

Joyce Conroy WHFC 91.1 FM
https://www.facebook.com/pages/911-FM-WHFC/120628751293977?pnref=lhc

The Ed O Neill Radio Show on Rocket Radio 95.3 Stockholm, Sweden
https://www.facebook.com/TheEdONeillradioshowonrocketradio95.3?fref=ts

Dave Smith Radio Presenter At Kennet Radio
https://www.facebook.com/KennetRadio?pnref=lhc

Bob Segarini "Don't Believe A Word I Say"
https://bobsegarini.wordpress.com

MY FAVORITE BANDS AND ARTISTS I'M LISTENING TO IN 2015

Go Wows, Palmyra Delran, Bang 74, Stupidity, New York Junk, Cynz, Hula Baby, Smoggers, Dahlmanns, The Moonstones, Nikki Corvette, Phil Shoenfelt. The Jellybricks. Room Full Of Strangers, Cheetah Chrome, The dB's, Screamin' Targets, Lannie Flowers, Laurie Biagini, Titty Twister, Roger Lewis.

FRANK SECICH DISCOGRAPHY

LPS AND CDS

Blue Ash - No More, No Less-1973 Mercury LP SRM1-666
Blue Ash - Front Page News-1977 LP PZ 34918
Stiv Bators - Disconnected-1980 Bomp! LP 4015 U.S., Canada, Finland, Germany
Stiv Bators - The Lord And The New Creatures LP France 1983
Infidels - Mad About That Girl 1985 LP France - Producer
Infidels - 9:25 And Seven Seconds-1987 LP - Producer
Infidels - Wondrous Strange-1989 CD - Producer
Stiv Bators - Stiv Bators/Night Of The Living Dead Boys-1989 Revenge 16/18 France
Dead Boys - Night Of The Living Dead Boys-Bonus Tracks-1994 Bomp!
Stiv Bators - L.A. L.A. 1994 Bomp! BCD 4046 U.S., Japan
Stiv Bators - Les Genies Du Rock (Sonic Reducer) 1994 Editions Atlas France
Blue Ash - Around Again-2004 Not Lame NL 093
Stiv Bators - Disconnected-25th Anniversary Edition-2004 Bomp! 4015-2
Stiv Bators - LA Confidential-2004 Bomp! BCD/LP 4089
Deadbeat Poets - Notes From The Underground 2007 Pop Detective CD U.S., Japan
Blue Ash - No More, No Less-2008 Collectors' Choice CD
Deadbeat Poets - Circustown-2010 CD Pop Detective
Deadbeat Poets - Youngstown Vortex Sutra (The British Version) CD-2011 Pop Detective
Deadbeat Poets - A Deadbeat Christmas-2011 CD Pop Detective
Deadbeat Poets - American Stroboscope-2012 CD Pop Detective
Deadbeat Poets - Hallelujah Anyway-2014 Lp/CD Pop Detective
Dead Boys - It's Cold Outside-2015 Double Live CD Time Bomb Records Japan
Deadbeat Poets - Strange Tales From The Hussman Building-2015 Pop Detective Records
Blue Ash - Hearts And Arrows - 2015 You Are The Cosmos-Spain 2 LP
Club Wow - Nowhere Fast - 2015 Zero Hour Records Australia (CD/DVD) + limited 45 'Prettiest Girl'

SINGLES AND EPS

Blue Ash - Abracadabra (Have You Seen Her?) b/w Dusty Old Fairgrounds 1973
Blue Ash - I Remember A Time b/w Plain To See 1973
Blue Ash - Anytime At All b/w She's So Nice 1974
Blue Ash - Look At You Now b/w Singing And Dancing Away 1977
Blue Ash - You Are All I Need b/w Jazel Jane 1977
Stiv Bators - It's Cold Outside b/w The Last Year 1979 U.S., England, Germany
Stiv Bators - Not That Way Anymore b/w Circumstantial Evidence 1980 U.S., Australia, Germany, Spain
Stiv Bators - Too Much To Dream b/w Make Up Your Mind 1981
Stiv Bators - Too Much To Dream-Newslines Vol. 1 EP 1981 Germany
Club Wow - Prettiest Girl b/w The Nights Are So Long - Criswell Records 1982
Infidels - Mad About That Girl b/w A Thousand Years Ago 1985 Producer
Infidels - The Infidels X 4 EP 1986 Producer
Infidels - I Can't Make You Mine b/w Everywhere I Go 1987 Producer
Dead Boys - All The Way Down (Poison Lady) b/w The Nights Are So Long 1987 Producer
Infidels - Run Away From You Flexi-Disc Hartbeat! #8 Germany 1988 Producer
Infidels - Final Solution Flexi-Disc Hartbeat! #9 Germany 1989 Producer
Dead Boys - It's All Right b/w War Zone 2000
Deadbeat Poets - Johnny Sincere-Pop Detective Records 2013

Stiv Bators & David Quinton - Make Up Your Mind- Ugly Pop Records 041 2013 Canada
Stiv Bators & Dead Boys - Last Stand 1980 EP- Ugly Pop Records 042 2013 Canada
Blue Ash 4 song 7" EP - You Are The Cosmos 2014 Spain
Deadbeat Poets - 7"EP - Joe The Mynah Bird, She's With Me. KOTJ Spain 2015

COMPILATIONS

Stiv Bators - It's Cold Outside. Rock Lines. Line LLP 5014 Germany 1979
Stiv Bators - It's Cold Outside. Yesterday's Sound Today Line Records Germany 1979
Stiv Bators - Circumstantial Evidence/I'll Be Alright. Where The Action Is!-Bomp! 1980
Stiv Bators - It's Cold Outside/The Last Year. Romantics And Friends-Quark Catch 3 1980
Stiv Bators - A Million Miles Away. Experiments In Destiny-Bomp! 4016 (2) 1980
Infidels - You Should See Yourself. We Can Work It Out-GMG 75018 France 1987 Producer
Hard Luck and Kashmyre - Love Only Me/47 Heaven. Scream Out Loud Vol. I 1987 Producer
Blue Ash - Dusty Old Fairgrounds. The Songs Of Bob Dylan-Start 20 England 1989
Infidels - Any Way You Want It. Munster Dance Hall Favorites Vol. III. Munster 003 Spain 1990 Producer
Blue Ash - Dusty Old Fairgrounds. I Shall Be Unreleased: The Songs Of Bob Dylan - Rhino 70518 1991
Stiv Bators - Boxed Set Of 5 Singles. I Wanna Be A Dead Boy- Munster 7029 Spain 1992
Stiv Bators - The Last Year. Destination Bomp!-Bomp! 4048 1994
Stiv Bators - It's Cold Outside" Revenge Records France 1995
Stiv Bators - Make Up Your Mind" The Roots Of Powerpop-Bomp! 1996
Blue Ash - Abracadabra (Have You Seen Her?) POPTOPIA! Power Pop Classics Of The '70's Rhino
    72728 1997 U.S., Japan
Blue Ash - Abracadabra (Have You Seen Her?). 100% Fun Power Pop Collection. Hiro 1001 Japan 1997
Stiv Bators - It's Cold Outside. Powerpearls Vol. 6 1999
Blue Ash - Anytime At All + 3. The History Of Powerpop Vol. 1 Cleveland 2000
Infidels - A Thousand Years Ago. Shake Some Action Vol. 2 SSA Records Spain 2001 Producer
Stiv Bators - Not That Way Anymore. Teenline # 7 Hyped-2-Death Records 2001
Stiv Bators - I'll Be Alright. Teenline #8 Hyped-2-Death Records 2003
Blue Ash - Pleasant Dreams. International Pop Overthrow Vol. 7 - Not Lame NL 101 2004
Blue Ash - Say Goodbye/She Cried For 15 Years. Planet Of The Popboomerang 2 Australia 2005
Infidels - Mad About That Girl. Home Runs Vol. 3 Sounds Asleep Records Sweden 2005 Producer
Stiv Bators - The Last Year. Home Runs Vol. 3 Sounds Asleep Records Sweden 2005
Dukes Of Earl - Him Or Me. He Put The Bomp! In The Bomp A Tribute To Greg Shaw Bomp/Vivid
    Sound Records U.S., Japan 2007 Producer/Artist
Deadbeat Poets - Ernest T. Unsigned, Sealed & Delivered-Frontline Records-2007 Canada
Deadbeat Poets - People These Days. IPO Vol. 13 Not Lame 2010
Deadbeat Poets - The Truth About Flying Saucers. Power Pop Prime Vol. 7 2011
Blue Ash - The Boy Won't Listen. Power Pop Prime Vol. 2 2012

SONGS RECORDED BY OTHER ARTISTS

A Million Miles Away (Secich) -Michael Monroe-Finland, Japan
A Million Miles Away (Secich) -Simon Chainsaw & The Forgotten Boys -Brazil
A Thousand Years Ago (Drivere-Secich) -The Infidels U.S., France, Spain
Abracadabra (Have You Seen Her?) (Secich-Bartolin) -The Records -England/USA
Crime In The Streets (Cabaniss-Quinton-Secich) -The Pop Machine
Don't Go Away (Zero-Secich) Stiv Bators -France
Everywhere I Go (Secich) -Infidels

Everywhere I Go (Secich) -Billy Sullivan
Evil Boy (Secich-Zero) -Stiv Bators & The Evil Boys -Germany
I Wanna Forget You (Just The Way You Are) (Secich-Bators) -Adam Bomb (Music) -U.S., UK
I'll Be Alright (Secich-Bators) -Hundred Million Martians -Finland
The Last Year (Secich-Bators) -The Monotors-Spain
The Last Year (Secich-Bators) -Palmflower
Not That Way Anymore (Secich-Bators) -Bad Luck Charms
Not That Way Anymore (Secich-Bators) -Road Vultures
Not That Way Anymore (Secich-Bators) -The Tragic Zeroes
Not That Way Anymore (Secich-Bators) -Starpower
Not That Way Anymore (Secich-Bators) -Nikki Sudden
The Girl Downstairs (Sullivan-Secich-Zero) -Billy Sullivan
Tonight's My Lucky Night (Secich-Bartolin) -Finkers-Australia
You Don't Go Away (Zero-Secich) -Vibeke Saugestad -Norway
You Don't Go Away (Zero-Secich) -Alpha Kitty

MUSIC VIDEOS

Who's Hieronymus Bosch & Why Is He Saying These Terrible Things About Me? -Deadbeat Poets 2012
Johnny Sincere -Deadbeat Poets -Pop Detective Records 2013

MUSIC IN FILMS

D.O.A. A Rite of Passage
Smother -2007 Official Trailer - Blue Ash -Can't Get Her Off My Mind
Return Of The Living Dead Boys - 2008- Bonus feature Interview Frank Secich and Stiv Bators
The Greenman 2011 - Directed by Joe Shelby -The Goody Wagon -The Green Man -Where Was I When I
                Needed Me? - Deadbeat Poets
Made In Cleveland 2013 - No Island Like The Mind, No Ship Like Beer -Deadbeat Poets

SPECIAL THANKS

Geoffrey Jones, Paul Nelson, Mark Hershberger, Gary Rhamy, John Hanti, John Grazier, Mark "Beaver' Warner, Bob Kierer, Eddy Best, Stiv Bators, Bill "Cupid" Bartolin, Boots Bell, David Quinton Steinberg, Mary Jean (Hurlbert) Volpe, Rita May Nickell, Ray Chizmar, Hank Frei, David Magnotto, Robbie and Elaina Duke, Joe Cvelbar, Anna Yendrek, Dianne Stephen, Chris Bell, Suzy Shaw, Patrick Boiselle, Oscar Garcia, Pedro Vizcaino, Barbie (Hyde) Stabile, Robert Knox Paxton, Bud Scoppa, Howard S. Berger, Bebe Buell, Jac Roblet, John Krizancic, Greg Shaw, Suzy Shaw, Paul Grant, Rich Schmidt, Jimmy Zero, Christopher Duda, Johnny Blitz, Cheetah Chrome, Larry Kennedy, Patryck Soubielle, John Cavanagh, Roger "Twiggy' Day, Johnny Kay, Kevin Avery, Ed Naha, Denice Bromley, Gary Kenton, Mark Generalovich, Mark Watkins, Dave Smith, Christine Ruffing, Joann (Rose) Liptak, Deirdre Gilmartin, Gail Goldberg Stoter, Bruce Brodeen, Smilja Raketich, Barry Dreyfus, Cynthia Ross, Joe Sztabnik, Hilary Hodgson, Dave Kaufman, Veronika Olivier, Kevin Kierer, Andrew Loog Oldham, Steven Van Zandt, Jane (Davis) Minton, Bob Mack, Merle Hauser, Brian Barry, Jacqui Dove, Doug Thomas, Gary McCoy, Gary Sloas, Roger Lewis, Palmyra Delran, Bill Kelly, Handsome "Dick" Manitoba, Mike Miller, Marty Magner, Steve Friedman, Mollie Lyon, Eric Bombeck, Leslie Bell Redman, Bill "Goog' Yendrek, Andy Gray, Barb Balchick, Regina Brazis Fabre, Joe "Lice' Harris, Newton Iliff, Haruko Shiozawa, Tsuneglam Sam, Steve Routman, Ken (Uncle Benny) Ondich, Jimmy Disko, Gayle Holland Morgado, Jo Chizmar Hanahan, Manfred Kodila, Mike Pinti, Tony Rossi, Lisa Bell Redman, Alyssa Ruffing, Jacob Ruffing, Nora Jones Daycak, Kirk Yano. Peanuts, Michael Versaci, Connie Dufford, Jeff Reding, Denise Dan Litton, Patty "Nugget" Hadley, Jim Pantelas, Scott Pickard, Ron Gordon, Rochelle Edwards Haas, Phyllis Nichols Abruzzino, Ken Sharp, John, Marcy Chizmar, Dave Schirmer, Barry Morley, Paula Heath, John Chizmar, Fran and Beth Kleja, Jeff Rozniata, Jim and Susan Kendzor, Jack Rielly, Darla Bartolin, Sean Bartolin, David Evans, Nora Jones Daycak, Frank and Dolly Secich, Geri Jones, Cindy (Secich) Wilpula, John Wilpula, Maryann (Secich) Hartmann, Jeff Rozniata, Brian Wingrove, Aleisa Drivere, Laurie Hartman, Bob Segarini, Steve Acker. Jackie Smelka, and George Matzkov from High Voltage Publishing/Zero Hour Records Australia.

www.ingramcontent.com/pod-product-compliance
Lightning Source LLC
LaVergne TN
LVHW041619070426
835507LV00008B/341